EMILY BRONTE
A Psychological Portrait

Emily Bronte

From a painting by Branwell Bronte

Emily Bronte

A PSYCHOLOGICAL PORTRAIT

BY

NORMA CRANDALL

RICHARD R. SMITH PUBLISHER, INC.

RINDGE, NEW HAMPSHIRE · 1957

KRAUS REPRINT CO.
New York
1970

Reprinted with the permission of the Licensor
KRAUS REPRINT CO.
A U.S. Division of Kraus-Thomson Organization Limited

Printed in U.S.A.

To

MARY V. AND WILLIAM E. HALL

FOREWORD

IN THE scarcity of authentic, first-hand material about Emily Bronte, many biographers necessarily have relied on theory. Vague theories about Emily's love life; her relations with her family, particularly with her brother, Branwell; about the real-life models in *Wuthering Heights* have replaced fact. It seems to the present writer that an authentic portrait of Emily Bronte, both as a person and as a writer can be drawn mainly by exploring the known facts about the lives and mentalities of the members of her family and by recreating the psychological atmosphere at Haworth Parsonage, Yorkshire, where Emily lived and wrote.

Emily Bronte, unlike Charlotte, hundreds of whose letters have been preserved, wrote very few letters. Not all of these have been preserved. With a few brief exceptions (Emily's few months in Roe Head School, at Miss Patchett's School and in the Pensionnat Heger in Brussels), Emily rarely penetrated beyond the Bronte family circle. Emily had very few friends and no definitely proven lovers. And, as a writer, many of her poems and *Wuthering Heights* originated in the complex network of these intimate family relations, which made up her emotional and spiritual environment. Hence, understanding the members of her family is not only the only certain method of portraying Emily, but is, because of her narrowly restricted life, essential in interpreting her writing. Indeed, it is the very core, bone and sinew of her creative motivation.

N. C.

New York, N. Y.
May, 1957

CONTENTS

ILLUSTRATIONS

Emily would never go . . . nothing would induce her into any sort of society, herself. "What is the use?" she said. "You will bring it all home to me."

—CHARLOTTE BRONTE

EMILY BRONTE
A Psychological Portrait

1

PATRICK BRONTE

AMONG the great writers of the past none is stranger by temperament or more paradoxical than the odd, intense moralist, the metaphysical poet and novelist Emily Bronte. No writer whose work is odder in its nature, streaked with greatness, yet narrowly limited, crude, even childlike. No writer in whom the creative processes and the emotional springs which fed them are more deeply hidden. No novelist of her time whose work has had more far-reaching repercussions. They still resound today.

Indeed, one can merely recreate Emily Bronte's personal life, so vividly moving in its primitive moorland setting and reverently seek clues. Nevertheless, much of the inner heart of this rare literary plant will remain obscure.

Emily Bronte's immediate family background was barely less remarkable or moving or even freakish than her own personality. Emily's mother died when Emily was three years old. But Patrick Bronte, Emily's father, an eccentric, peasant-born, Irish, Church of England clergyman was nearly as interesting a human being as his celebrated children. The combination of Mr. Bronte's temperament with his early, brilliant, hard-won rise in the world and his subsequent partial frustration created an eccentric parental background for Emily.

In reality, perhaps as a result of an obscure, unrecorded experience in Emily's childhood, Mr. Bronte was probably unwittingly partly responsible for the fact that Emily's real life remained primarily an interior one.

Patrick Bronte was born on St. Patrick's Day in 1777 in a two-room peasant hut in a tiny North of Ireland village named Emdale in County Down. Patrick was the eldest of ten children of a Protestant peasant farmer, Hugh Brunty and Elinor McCloy, a Catholic who became a Protestant when she married Mr. Brunty.

In his boyhood, Patrick had been intensely ambitious and precociously brilliant. At the end of a twelve-hour day as a weaver, Patrick devoted his nights to study. Only sixteen, Mr. Bronte had been appointed a master in a local Presbyterian school, Glascar Hill. At twenty-one he was already a parish school principal in Drumballyroney.

Mr. Bronte's subsequent rise from an obscure parish schoolmaster to a Church of England clergyman had resulted from sheer inner determination, moral courage and scholarly ability. Morally encouraged by his parish vicar, Patrick determined to enter Cambridge, one of England's two great universities for her most distinguished sons, as a divinity student. Patrick Bronte, with only seven pounds, and no prospect of a university scholarship, departed for England at the age of twenty-five.

A noted Cornish missionary, a Mr. Henry Martyn, has left a revealing, piquant and rather dramatic portrait of young Mr. Bronte at Cambridge University. Mr. Martyn had written to a religious philanthropist for funds for the young divinity student to add to the scholarships (or exhibitions) which Mr. Bronte had already won. Mr. Martyn emphasized both Mr. Bronte's unconventional daring and his dedication.

> He (Mr. Bronte) has given me some account of his outset to college, which for its singularity has hardly been equalled. He left his native Ireland with seven pounds, then received an unexpected supply of five pounds from a distant friend . . . Since, no other aid, but what the college afforded . . . There is reason to hope that he will be an

instrument of good to the Church, as a desire of usefulness in the ministry seems to have influenced him in no small degree.*

Ordained in London in 1806, Mr. Bronte finally settled in Haworth, Yorkshire as permanent curate in 1821.

* For sources of quoted material see "Materials and Sources."

2

EMILY'S EARLY BACKGROUND
IN HAWORTH, YORKSHIRE

In a remote moorland, Yorkshire manse, Emily Bronte's early years probably very much resembled those of her heroine, Cathy Earnshaw, in *Wuthering Heights*. Emily, like Cathy, was emotionally isolated and often alone on the moors, psychically alienated from her elders: Mr. Bronte and the late Mrs. Bronte's sister, Aunt Branwell.

Surely Emily's emotional intensity was rooted not only in the strong and eccentric Bronte temperament but also in a natural environment which inevitably heightened the inner imaginative life. Certainly the rugged, grand moorland landscape, which Emily described so beautifully in her novel, deepened the emotions and reduced the pedestrian realities of ordinary, everyday living to minor perspective, creating much the same mood that it did in her novel.

Haworth, a nearly medieval town, mentioned in the Domesday Book, straggled up a steep moorland hillside, high in the grim, barren, gritstone Yorkshire hills. It was set on the very edge of a seemingly endless moorland plateau, which with the seasons, was either snow- and rain-swept or purple-heather-blooming and bird-infested. The nearest sizable town, Keighley, was four miles distant—reachable only on foot or in Haworth's unique, hired gig. Railroads did not penetrate this Yorkshire district until Emily was in her teens.

Haworth Parsonage, on the peak of Haworth Hill, sur-

4

rounded by a scrubby thorn and currant bush garden, edged the moorland plateau. In the rear, in Emily Bronte's words a:

> Little and a lone green lane
> That opened on a common wide

led directly to the moors.

Yet, the Georgian, slate-roofed, stone manse, in which Emily grew up, which bordered Haworth Cemetery separating the manse from Haworth Church, was not provincially dingy. In the memories of Charlotte Bronte's biographer, Mrs. Gaskell, and Charlotte's friend, Ellen Nussey, the interior had a certain charm. The manse's tall, French windows, high-mantelled fireplaces, recessed bookcases, polished mahogany furniture and stone floors and dove-grey walls made an impression of elegant ease.

But otherwise Emily Bronte's rural isolation (like Cathy Earnshaw's in *Wuthering Heights*) was complete. Haworth, a small industrial town, was one of the new, West Riding wool and cloth manufacturing centers which had absorbed the ancient, peasant hand-weaving industry, as steam and water power replaced hand looms in the rise of the Industrial Revolution.

Yorkshire, with its poor roads and interminable winter, had remained so primitive that the brutalities which Emily melodramatized almost morbidly in her novel were matched by local bull-baitings, cockfights and drunken horseraces. One remembers Mrs. Gaskell's description of a typical Yorkshire squire who had watched a cockfight on his deathbed, aided by mirrors, undisturbed by his own approaching death. Haworth funeral feasts ("Arvills") usually ended in the imprisonment of the drunken mourners.

Yet the bleak, withdrawn quality of the Brontes' lives in Haworth, which deeply affected Emily, also had psychic roots. In Haworth, Mr. Bronte had become a probably embittered and certainly a frustrated man. Here, a harsh, narrow-minded strain in Mr. Bronte's nature had been intensified by tragedy and disappointment.

Mrs. Bronte had died tragically from an internal cancer about a year and a half after she and her husband had settled in Haworth—in September, 1821. Patrick Bronte had been left not merely with his grief but with the difficult problem of rearing his six tiny children: Maria and Elizabeth Bronte aged eight and seven, born in Hartshead, Yorkshire, and Charlotte, aged five, Patrick Branwell, four, Emily Jane, three and Anne, a one-year old baby, born in Thornton, Yorkshire.

Despite Mr. and Mrs. Bronte's different temperaments and backgrounds, they had achieved a measure of happiness. Maria Branwell Bronte came from an upper-middle-class, civically and religiously prominent family in Penzance, Cornwall. When Patrick Bronte was a curate in Hartshead, Yorkshire, he had married Miss Branwell during a holiday visit to her Branwell aunt, Mrs. Fennel, whose husband was headmaster of a Methodist college, near Leeds.

Emily Bronte's mother, from her letters and her evangelical essay: "The Advantages of Poverty in Religious Concerns," had been a gentle, pious soul. Apparently Mrs. Bronte had retained a lingering nostalgia for her native Cornwall. Mrs. Gaskell stated that when Mrs. Bronte was dying, she delighted in watching the maid clean the fire-grate because: "She did it as it was done in Cornwall." Yet Mrs. Bronte's last words spoken to a maid were, according to Mrs. Gaskell, "Ought I not to be thankful he (Mr. Bronte) never gave me an angry word?"

Mr. Bronte had been deeply, perhaps permanently, shaken by his wife's death. Writing to his former vicar, the Vicar of Dewsbury, Mr. Bronte stated:

Tender sorrow was my daily portion—oppressive grief sometimes lay heavy—when an affectionate, agonizing something sickened my whole frame—I missed her at every corner—her memory hourly revived by the distressing prattle of my children.

Furthermore, Mr. Bronte was a disappointed writer. During his nine-year marriage, Mr. Bronte had published three books: *The Rural Minstrel,* a book of religious poetry (a first volume had been published previously); and two novels: *Cottage In The Wood* and *The Maid of Illarney.*

Mr. Bronte knew his literary limitations. Yet writing was essential to Mr. Bronte's inner happiness. As he movingly explained:

> When relieved from clerical avocations, he was occupied in writing "The Cottage Poems." From morning to noon and from noon till night, his employment was full of indescribable pleasure, such as he could wish to taste as long as life lasts. His hours glided pleasantly and almost imperceptibly by, and when night drew on, and he retired to rest, ere his eyes closed in sleep with sweet calmness and serenity of mind, he often reflected that, though the delicate palate of criticism might be disgusted . . . his humble task was well pleasing in the sight of God and might be useful to some poor soul who cared little for critical niceties.

Hence as Mr. Bronte wrote to his Thornton friend, Miss Firth, "The Thornton years were my happiest."

But Patrick Bronte was not the inhuman, almost sadistic father portrayed by Mrs. Gaskell. As Mr. Bronte, with rare self-perception, wrote to Mrs. Gaskell in self-defense when her book was published:

> I do not deny that I am somewhat eccentric. Had I been numbered among the calm, sedate concentric men of the world, I should not have been as I now am, and, I should in all probability never have had such children as mine have been— Only don't set me on in my fury to burning

up hearth rugs; sawing the backs of chairs; and tearing up my wife's silk gowns.

Even Mrs. Gaskell admitted that despite his "misanthropy, yet not one of his opinions could be modified by any worldly motive."

And, according to Charlotte's intimate friend, Miss Nussey, he was an admirable and revered clergyman. As Miss Nussey explained:

The Sexton, with a long staff, knobbed sleepers awake. But when the sermon began there was a change. Attitudes took listening forms, eyes were turned on the preacher. Mr. Bronte addressed his hearers in extemporare style. Very often he selected a parable from one of the Gospels —which he later explained in the simplest manner—so as to be perfectly intelligible to the lowest comprehension.

But in Haworth Mr. Bronte, selfishly ingrown, even ill, lived, as he admitted to Miss Firth in 1835:

A stranger in a strange land. In this place I have received civilities and I have, I trust, been civil to all, but I have not tried to make any new friends, nor have I met with any whose minds were congenial to my own.

At the parsonage, Mr. Bronte, blaming a digestive disorder probably psychosomatic dined alone in his study. As he explained to Miss Firth:

My own health is but very delicate—with great care, I am able to perform my ministerial duties. Indeed, I *have* not been well since I left Thornton.

Yet, despite Mr. Bronte's self-preoccupation, when Emily was a child, he had moments of fatherly tendresse. In a sermon, Mr. Bronte movingly recalled his emotional anxiety about Emily, Branwell and Anne during a thunderstorm:

On the second day of September, 1824, at about six o'clock in the afternoon, two portions of the moors sank several yards during a heavy storm of thunder, lightning and rain, and there issued forth a mighty volume of mud and water which spread alarm, astonishment, and danger along its course of many miles . . . As the day was exceedingly fine I had sent my little children who were indisposed, accompanied by the servants, to take an airing on the common, and as they stayed longer than I expected, I mounted to an upper chamber to look for their safe return. The heavens were blackening fast . . . my little family had escaped to a place of safety but I did not know it. I consequently watched every movement with a painful degree of interest.

It was Mr. Bronte who gave his children the toy soldiers who became the central characters in their earliest writings. Mr. Bronte, returning late one evening from a trip to Leeds, had awakened Branwell, to give him a requested box of wooden soldiers.

Yet, on the whole, Emily Bronte's early years were probably clouded by fear, restraint and repression. For Mr. Bronte ruled his children's lives with an iron hand. Partially frustrated himself, and believing that his children, in his words, showed "signs of rising talent," he became tyrannical.

When Charlotte, then a famous novelist, asked Mr. Bronte's permission to marry his curate, Mr. Nicholls (whom she later did marry), he had raged abuse against Mr. Nicholls, until as Charlotte wrote to a friend, she feared an apoplectic stroke. Perhaps even more revealing of Mr. Bronte's relations with his children, as Charlotte once told this same friend, "Compassion or relenting is no more to be looked for from Papa than sap from firewood."

When Emily was a child, Mr. Bronte probably inspired an unreasoning fear. Certainly Mr. Bronte's test of his little children's minds was not only eccentric but indicates how deeply he was feared. As he later recalled the incident to Mrs. Gaskell:

> In order to make them speak with less timidity, and happening to have a mask in the house, I told them to stand back and speak boldly from under cover of the mask.

Emily, who, as it happened, had been asked by her father, "What had I best do with your brother Branwell who is often a naughty boy," had replied with her characteristic directness and simplicity, "Reason with him and when he won't listen to reason, whip him."

But the fear which Mr. Bronte instilled into the atmosphere at the parsonage was usually manifested more indirectly. When Emily was about six years old, Mr. Bronte preached a sermon in which he identified a local thunderstorm with Hellfire:

> The torrents of mud and water were awful proof that it was an irresistable instrument to execute His final judgment.

And Charlotte claimed that she

> Never remembers her Father dressing himself in the morning without putting a loaded pistol in his pocket—the pistol sitting down to breakfast with us.

To Emily Bronte, Mr. Bronte must have seemed inhuman if not repellent.

It was particularly unfortunate that Emily had virtually no mother. Mr. Bronte admired his late wife's sister, Miss Branwell, who had nursed the dying Mrs. Bronte and had remained in Haworth to bring up her nieces and nephew. To a friend, Mr. Bronte described Aunt Branwell as "an affectionate Mother to my children and a consolation to me sharing my labours and sorrows."

But, actually, Aunt Branwell reared her nieces, particularly Emily and Charlotte, as a matter of duty. Between Emily and Aunt Branwell, there was neither deep understanding, or love or shared interests. A prim, Methodist spinster, Aunt Branwell, according to Charlotte's friends, Miss Nussey and Miss Taylor, carefully trained her nieces, as Miss Taylor wrote, in, "morals, manners and deportment." And, in domestic tasks "she made her nieces sew and discouraged any other culture."

Miss Branwell delighted in the melodramatic thriller novels in the already outdated "ladies' magazines." As Charlotte later explained to William Wordsworth, "She (Aunt) thinks them superior to any trash of modern literature."

To Aunt Branwell, it was, perhaps, her only means of escape from dreary duty. In bleak Yorkshire, Aunt lived (Miss Nussey tells us) mostly in her bedroom and, mentally, in a dim, never-never land, midway between her present reality and nostalgic memories of balmy-climated, sociable Penzance, Cornwall, where Aunt had once been a belle.

According to Miss Nussey, Miss Branwell, a tiny, meticulously black-silk-gowned, Cornish gentlewoman, wearing huge silk caps and taking snuff from a gold case, clattered about the parsonage in her wooden pattens with unconcealed distaste. Apparently, Aunt remained a disgruntled alien in Yorkshire. But (except for Miss Nussey's incisive portrait), Aunt Branwell is like a shadowy figure in a faded portrait whose features one discerns just clearly enough to realize that they are unexceptional.

Aunt's influence on Emily was probably as ineffectual as it was on Charlotte. When Aunt died, Charlotte, who, Miss Taylor stated, never mentioned her Aunt, had commented with astonishing matter-of-factness, "Aunt is gone. We shall see her no more." Emily's feelings were probably also tinged with scorn. Emily referred to Methodists in her novel as "ranting," "Hypocritical," etc.

Only Anne and certainly Branwell ("Aunt's favorite") found maternal qualities in Aunt Branwell. As Branwell wrote to a friend about Aunt's death—though perhaps with a touch of his usual emotional self-dramatization:

> Your sister would not blame me now for indulging in gloomy visions. I have lost the guide and director of all the happy days connected with my childhood.

Emily found in Tabitha Ackroyd, the parsonage house-keeper who came to the manse when Emily was seven years old, the warm motherly qualities, which she needed and lacked. In the parsonage kitchen, Taby (like Nelly Dean in *Wuthering Heights*) sang Yorkshire ballads and told Yorkshire tales in broad dialect. In one's mind's eye, one sees Emily seated in front of the parsonage kitchen fire, with a book or a paper and pencil (much as she described herself later in a diary) listening to Taby, avidly absorbing the details of Yorkshire life. As Charlotte explained:

> Though Emily's feeling for the people round was benevolent, intercourse with them she never sought; nor, with very few exceptions, ever experienced. And, yet she knew their ways; their language; their family histories; she could hear of them with interest, and talk of them with detail, minute, graphic, and accurate; but WITH them she rarely exchanged a word. This knowledge resulted from listening to the secret annals of every rude vicinage.

Actually, Emily's first adventure in the world beyond Haworth was not propitious. The barriers were nearly insurmountable. Emily had almost no opportunity of enriching the rather sketchy human background at the parsonage. Perhaps because Mr. Bronte's first experience with local boarding schools had been tragic (Maria and Elizabeth Bronte had died following a school typhoid epidemic) Emily, except for a few months at the age of six, did not again leave Haworth to attend boarding school until adolescence.

Emily Bronte's few months at The Clergy Daughters' School during her sixth winter (where Maria and Elizabeth Bronte had preceded her in July and Charlotte in August) are meagerly recorded. The school registry reports:

Entered November 25th, 1824. Aged 6-1/2. Reads very prettily and works a little. Left June 1, 1825. Subsequent career, Governess.

Yet an unrecorded experience here could easily have partly motivated Emily's lifelong, almost pathological dread of the world beyond Haworth. The Clergy Daughters' School at Cowan Bridge was a morbid institution pervaded by a sadistic, religious fanaticism. If the religious magazine for children, which the school's headmaster, Rev. W. C. Wilson, edited, reflects the treatment meted to pupils, it seems doubtful that even six-year-old Emily could escape without a permanent psychic scar. Mr. Wilson's (Charlotte's Black Marble Clergyman of Lowood School in *Jane Eyre*) magazine was devoted to hair-raising descriptions, verbal and pictorial, of hangings, massacres, deaths which God inflicted on unruly children. In one such tale, a small child is struck dead for a minor misdemeanor, without even "time to pray." In another tale, a three-and-a-half-year-old boy, asked whether he preferred life or death, had replied, "Death for me."

In reality, death was in the air at this unpleasant school. Because of the location, in a damp, low-lying river valley, the dank, unheated stone buildings and the poor, even rancid, food there were frequent low fever (typhoid) epidemics. During one of these, Emily's two elder sisters were sent home, in February and in May, to die shortly afterwards. Finally, in June, Mr. Bronte withdrew Emily and Charlotte.

Emily's education was resumed in the more tranquil atmosphere of the parsonage under the tutelage of Aunt Branwell and Mr. Bronte.

3

EMILY IN ADOLESCENCE

IN ADOLESCENCE, Emily lives intensely, if obliquely, in minute bird's-eye views: in scraps of Charlotte's letters and diaries; in Emily's own diary fragment, written jointly with Anne. But above all in the written memories of Charlotte's two intimate friends, whom Charlotte met at Roe Head Boarding School, Mary Taylor and Ellen Nussey.

Charlotte's lifelong friendship with these two young ladies began when Charlotte was fifteen years old. Miss Nussey and Miss Taylor remained primarily Charlotte's friends. But they played an important, if indirect, role in Emily's life. They provided all the Brontes with mental vistas of worlds beyond Haworth. They were avenues of exit for Emily and Charlotte from their narrow province. Miss Taylor was largely responsible for the fact that Emily and Charlotte spent nine months in Brussels in their twenties. But, above all, these two ladies provide present-day Bronte readers with telescopic lenses through time which enable us to view Emily and the Brontes, unposed, unobserved, moving about the parsonage in the intimate privacy of their daily lives. Both Miss Nussey and Miss Taylor kept detailed diaries.

Despite a wide mental gap between Ellen Nussey and the Bronte sisters, Charlotte, at least, was perhaps emotionally fonder of Ellen than of Mary Taylor. In Ellen, Charlotte evidently found a healing normality and moral stability. Charlotte, writing years later to her editor and friend, Mr. Williams, explained:

When I first saw Ellen, I did not care for her. We were contrasts—still we suited. Now no new friend, however lofty or profound in intellect could be to me what Ellen is; yet she is no more than a conscientious, observant, calm, well-bred Yorkshire girl. She is without romance (or poetry). But she is good; she is true; she is faithful; and I love her.

Apparently Emily and Anne agreed. Charlotte, writing to Ellen after one of the latter's various parsonage visits, stated, "They (Emily and Anne) never saw anyone they liked so well as you."

Yet Mary Taylor was the Bronte sisters' intellectual equal. Liberal-minded and progressive, Miss Taylor, the daughter of a nonconformist textile manufacturer, later daringly emigrated to New Zealand where she founded a dry-goods business. Later, in England, she published two books, a novel and a work on women's rights. To Charlotte, Miss Taylor represented, in Charlotte's words, "My model for intellectual and moral daring."

In remembering Charlotte in Roe Head School, Miss Nussey and Miss Taylor have created a moving portrait which very much prefigures Emily's experience in the same school a few years later. Charlotte's experience, like Emily's, was an unequal battle between an inwardly self-preoccupied, intensely individual individual and what invariably appeared to the Brontes to be an arbitrary, alien world of reality.

The Misses Wooler's private boarding school, where Charlotte was a pupil for a year and a half (1831-32) was a small, semifashionable finishing school of about ten pupils. In this prim, genteel milieu, Charlotte, self-conscious and introspective, from what she herself described as a "wild, moorland village," was an odd, yet definitely respected, figure.

In her friends' reminiscences Charlotte was a diminutive, near-sighted adolescent who refused to join her classmates' games, preferring to sit quietly under a shaded tree and peer intently at the sky and landscape; who had a disquieting tendency to weep silently in the schoolroom in the late afternoon dusk or to kneel near a window doing "double lessons" until her fellow-pupils accused her of "seeing in the dark." She had a phenomenal knowledge of literature and politics, yet she lacked an elementary education. Apparently she had a strange predilection for impersonating eerie characters in her own self-devised ghost stories at night, so realistically that it seriously disturbed her fellow-pupils. Charlotte was eventually reprimanded and fined.

But Charlotte, temperamentally isolated and emotionally an alien (except for two friends) in Roe Head, was obviously torn by nostalgia for Haworth Parsonage and particularly for composing tales and poems about the imaginary world of Angria with Branwell. In a letter she described an afternoon visit from Branwell as an ecstatic oasis in an otherwise unbearably dreary existence.

Miss Nussey first visited Haworth Parsonage when Emily was fifteen. It was a return visit to Charlotte who the previous September had been Ellen's guest at the latter's home in Birstall, seventeen miles from Haworth. Miss Nussey's large, battlemented manor house, with its rookery and cultivated gardens, must have seemed a realized dream to Charlotte with her romantic imagination. Branwell, who had escorted Charlotte to Birstall, probably echoed Charlotte's delight, when he remarked: "I am leaving you in Paradise."

After various delays, Ellen reached the parsonage the end of August (1833). The visit had been deferred, because as Charlotte had written to Ellen in June:

> Aunt thought it would be better to defer it until about the middle of summer, as the winter, and even the spring seasons are remarkably cold and bleak among our mountains.

In Ellen's impression of Emily, Emily's deepest traits, her passion for nature, her reserve, her inward fire, were then emerging, along with her basic, family patterns.

Physically, Emily was, in Miss Nussey's words:

> The tallest person in the house except her father. She had a lithesome, graceful figure. Her hair, as naturally beautiful as Charlotte's, was in the same unbecoming tight curl and frizz and there was the same want of complexion . . . She had very beautiful eyes, kind, kindling, liquid eyes—their color might be said to be dark grey, at other times, blue, they varied so. But she did not often look at you. She was too reserved.

Yet, as Miss Nussey later wrote to Mrs. Gaskell:

> Few people have the gift of looking and smiling as Emily could smile. One of her rare expressive looks was something to remember through life, there was such a depth of soul and feeling, yet such a shyness of revealing herself— a strength of self-containment seen in no other . . . [and] talked very little.

But, in the heart of the moorland Emily, when released from the parsonage:

> Her reserve was replaced by naive delight. On top of a moor or in a deep glen, Emily became a child for glee and enjoyment. In fine suitable weather rambles were made over the moor and down into glens and ravines that broke the monotony of the moorland. The rugged bank and rippling brook were treasures of delight. The Brontes forded streams, sometimes placing stepping stones . . . there was always a lingering delight in these sports . . . every flower, every tint, and form were noted and enjoyed. Emily especially had a delight in these nooks of beauty . . . her reserve for the time being vanished.

According to both Miss Nussey and Charlotte, Emily passionately identified herself with the timeless, impersonal grandeur of nature. It became increasingly an inner balance wheel—a healing refuge from her tormented inner life—the heart of her mystic faith. As Emily wrote:

> The earth that wakes ONE human heart to feeling can centre both the worlds of Heaven and Hell.

And as Charlotte later explained in her Preface to *Wuthering Heights*:

> Ellis Bell did not describe nature as one whose eyes and taste alone found pleasure in the prospect; her native hills were far more to her than a spectacle; they were what she lived in and by, as much as the wild birds, their tenants, or as the heather, their produce.

And as Miss Nussey recalled:

> What the Brontes cared for and lived in most were the surroundings of nature. The green expanse of hill and mountain, the purple heather, the dells and glens, and brooks, the broad sky view, the whistling winds, the snowy expanse, the starry heavens and the charm of that solitude and seclusion which sees things from a distance without the disturbing atmosphere which lesser minds are apt to create.

Even the tiny, scraggy parsonage garden was devotedly tended by Emily and Anne.

> The garden, which, nearly all grass and possessed only a few stunted thorns, shrubs and a few currant bushes which Emily and Anne treasured as their own bit of fruit garden.

Nature was now also a theme for philosophizing. In a moorland retreat, Emily brooded on the moral values in human destiny. Miss Nussey recalled a rustic outing to a favorite

Bronte retreat which the Brontes named "The Meeting of the Waters."

It was a small oasis of emerald green turf, broken here and there by small, clear springs; a few large stones served as resting places; seated here we were hidden from all the world, nothing appearing in view but miles and miles of heather, a glorious blue sky and brightening sun . . . a fresh breeze wafted its exhilarating influence . . . we made mirth of each other. But Emily, reclining on a slab of stone, played like a young child with tadpoles in the water, making them swim about and then fell to moralizing on the strong and the weak, the brave and the cowardly, as she chased them with her hand.

Emily was closer to Anne than to Charlotte. Emily and Anne were, in Miss Nussey's words, "Like twins, inseparable companions . . . in the very closest sympathy which never had any interruption." Yet, Anne was the most pedestrian of the Brontes. Miss Nussey writes:

Her hair was a very pretty light brown and fell on her neck in graceful curls. She had lovely, violet-blue eyes, fine pencilled eyebrows and a clear, almost transparent complexion . . . she still pursued her studies under her aunt, especially her sewing . . . she played also but she preferred soft harmonies and vocal music. She sang a little; her voice was weak, but very sweet in tone.

But Emily and Anne had deep bonds. They shared a love of music. Ellen Nussey tells us that Emily, who was taught piano playing by the Keighley organist, played with "brilliance and precision."

Emily and Anne were both immersed in writing tales and poems about the imaginary world of Gondal and they were both innately retiring. Charlotte described Anne when the latter became a governess as a "patient, persecuted stranger.

She is less gifted with the power of making friends than I am, more lonely." Emily was equally unsociable and hermitic. Charlotte writes:

> Emily would never go . . . nothing would induce her into any sort of society, herself. "What is the use?" she said. "You will bring it all home to me."

Between Emily and Charlotte there was an obvious cleavage in temperament. Miss Nussey had related an apparently trivial incident, which yet flashes a telltale light on the relations between the two sisters. When Ellen had returned from a moorland ramble with Emily (who, writes Miss Nussey, "liked me for I never seemed to remark her peculiarities"), Charlotte had asked her friend: "And Emily, how did she behave?" And, in a similar vein, Charlotte, writing years later to her former schoolmistress, Miss Wooler, said of Emily: "I wish Emily were not quite so intractable, more open to reason." And there was "the certain harshness in my sister's nature," about which Charlotte complained. (It was, perhaps, this hardness which once permitted Emily, when she was bitten by a dog with hydrophobia, to cauterize her wound with a hot iron—an incident which Charlotte dramatized in her novel, *Shirley*, which was based on Emily, and which she told Mrs. Gaskell was true.)

Ellen Nussey also described another, apparently unimportant incident in the relations between Emily and Charlotte which yet has an odd ring. One wonders what hidden motives induced Emily, in Miss Nussey's words, to:

> . . . delight in leading Charlotte where she would not go of her own free will. Charlotte had a mortal dread of unknown animals, and it was Emily's pleasure to lead her into their close vicinity and then to tell her, laughing at her horror.

Emily probably resented her elder sister. One suspects that

she repressed a dislike of the fact that Charlotte, in many respects, dominated her younger sisters. Charlotte was both far more ambitious—and capable—in a material sense than Emily. As Charlotte once wrote to Aunt Branwell, "I want us all to get on." But Emily had none of Charlotte's aggressiveness. One remembers Emily's lines, perhaps written with Charlotte in mind:

And leaving busy chase of wealth and learning
For idle dreams of things which cannot be.

Yet Emily and Anne's practical lives were entirely dominated by Charlotte's ambitions. Charlotte paid Emily's (and later Anne's) tuition in boarding school by teaching. Charlotte evolved a plan whereby the three sisters could become financially independent, by starting a private school. Charlotte arranged for and borrowed the necessary money from Aunt Branwell, to enable herself and Emily to study in Brussels. Charlotte, when they were studying drawing with the Leeds portrait painter, William Robinson, who taught them at the parsonage, envisioned that they might become professional painters. Charlotte, when she returned to Haworth from Roe Head, undertook to educate her younger sisters. As Charlotte wrote to Ellen, "In the mornings I instruct my sisters and draw, etc." Finally, Charlotte was responsible for Emily's initial appearance in print. It was Charlotte who, when she accidentally discovered Emily's poetry notebook, practically forced Emily to agree to publish her poems in a joint book of poetry by the three sisters. Probably Charlotte arranged for the sisters to join a local library; the Mechanics' Institute in Keighley. It was a vital supplement to the sketchy parsonage library; an assortment of religious books, odd classics, the Romantic Poets, Sir Walter Scott's works, etc.

Emily might easily have felt herself unpleasantly overshadowed by her more competent and able elder sister—to whom in less outwardly visible ways, she must have realized she was superior.

But whatever Emily's inner feelings, she only expressed independence on a purely mental plane. Mary Taylor stated that when Emily and Charlotte were sight-seeing in the London art galleries, in matters of aesthetic taste "Emily never took her (Charlotte's) opinion but always had one to offer." And Emily was much less intimidated by her father's and her Aunt's Hellfire and Eternal Damnation religious orthodoxy than Branwell and her two sisters, to whom it remained a lifelong torment. Mary Taylor remembered that once during a parsonage visit:

> I mentioned that someone has asked me what religion I was (with a view to getting me for a partisan). I had said that was between God and me. Emily, who was lying on the hearth rug, exclaimed: "That's right." This was all I ever heard Emily say on religious subjects . . .

But otherwise, Emily's development as a human being remained freakishly unequal to her inner, spiritual growth. Despite her inward fire, she was, either naturally or because of the isolation in which she lived or was forced to remain by family tensions and repressions, unbelievably emotionally immature. It seems incredible that Emily was actually sixteen when the following diary was written:

Emily Jane Bronte——Anne Bronte

I fed Rainbow, Diamond, Snowflake, Jaspar Pheasant (alias). This morning Branwell went down to Mr. Driver's and brought news that Sir Robert Peel was going to be invited to stand for Leeds. Anne and I have been peeling apples for Charlotte to make a pudding and for Aunt's . . . Charlotte said that she made puddings perfectly and she. . . . of quick but limited intellect. Taby said just now Come Anne pilloputate. Aunt had come into the kitchen just now and said Where are your feet Anne Anne answered on the floor Aunt. Papa opened the parlour door and gave Branwell a letter saying Here Branwell read this and show it to your Aunt and Charlotte. The Gondals are discovering the interior of Gaaldine. Sally Mosely is washing in the back kitchen.

It is past twelve o'clock anne and I have not tidied ourselves, done our bedwork, or done our lessons and we want to go out to play. We are going to have for dinner Boiled Beef, Turnips potatoes and apple pudding. The kitchen is in a very untidy state Anne and I have not done our music exercise which consists of B Major Taby said on my putting a pen in her face Ya pitter pottering there instead of pilling a potatoe I answered O dear O dear O dear I will derectly With that I get up, take aknife and begin pilling. Finished pilling the potatoes Papa going for a walk Mr. Sunderland expected.

Anne and I say I wonder what we shall be like and what we shall be and where we shall be, if all goes well, in the year 1874 in which year I shall be in my 57th year. Anne will be in her 55th year Branwell will be going on his 58th year and Charlotte in her 59th year Hoping we shall all be well at that time We close our paper.

November 24, 1834.

4

EMILY AND BRANWELL

T HE NOTE of ugly melodrama which Branwell introduced into the Brontes' lives at the tranquil parsonage was sounded early. When Emily was still in her teens, his tragic future was apparent.

If Charlotte's ambitions were resented by Emily, Branwell was the source of a lifelong, inner torment.

In Branwell's final tragedy, there were reasons both in his upbringing and in his temperament. It seems to this writer that the combination of these two made the end result inevitable. Among the more obvious causes were his lax, undisciplined upbringing; the scattering of his undoubted real talents in three arts: music, painting, and literature; the necessary application in none; family adulation; the unreasonably high hopes held for him by his family and by his friends. But, perhaps most important, was his own lack of clarity about the true nature of his talent. Branwell's true gift was that of a minor poet. It was in poetry that he later on achieved his only real artistic success. But whatever the exact causes, the innate talent, with which Branwell in common with his three sisters had been originally endowed, was destroyed, early.

Branwell, indulged by Mr. Bronte ("My only son," as Mr. Bronte lamented when Branwell died) and by Aunt Branwell, with whom he was "a great favorite," had been, as he himself eventually realized in explaining his failure: "too much petted in life." Yet Branwell was denied the normal friendships of boyhood, except for those of mentally inferior

Branwell Bronte

From a drawing by Miss E. Taylor

village lads, with whom Branwell in turn, because of his short height, felt physically uneasy, as Charlotte claimed. Charlotte stated that her brother's lifelong interest in prize fighters and in prize fighting was an attempt to compensate for physical inferiority. Handsome (Charlotte described Branwell to her editor friend as the "handsomest" member of her family), and an eloquent talker, he was a fascinating companion, according to his friends.

In Haworth, in his teens, Branwell divided his energies among pursuit of the three arts: writing—collaborating with Charlotte on tales about the imaginary world of Angria—music and portrait painting. He also drank heavily at the local inn. Branwell both played the flute and took organ lessons from the Keighley organist. A Haworth villager has reported that in the early dusk organ strains could be heard in the town as Branwell practiced in Mr. Bronte's dark, empty church.

But Branwell, from about the age of seventeen until a few days before he died, shared moments of intoxication with a passing commercial traveller or brilliantly monologued over a few drinks with a Haworth friend, at The Black Bull Inn. Unfortunately, here Branwell invariably found a ready and willing audience, including Mr. Bronte's sexton, John Brown, whose two daughters later became parsonage maids.

In Charlotte's thinly disguised sketches of Branwell, in her early tales, the character traits which now motivated his alcoholism and eventually destroyed him are very apparent. In Charlotte's stories, Branwell, vainglorious and self-dramatizing, is already a flamboyant egomaniac. During the next few years, Branwell was to express this egomania, in real life, in the melodramatic, dictatorial, self-glorifying letters with which he angrily bombarded leading contemporary writers and editors—particularly the editors of *Blackwood's Magazine*. But unfortunately a romantic nature and a dramatic sense of personal importance, though often part of the artistic temperament, are not, necessarily, by themselves a gauge of creative ability.

Charlotte, in an introduction to one of her Angrian tales, written when Branwell was seventeen, penetratingly satirized Branwell, both physically and psychologically:

A low, slightly built man in a black coat and raven grey trousers, his hat placed nearly at the back of his head, revealing a bush of carrotty hair so arranged that at the sides it projected almost like two spread hands, a pair of spectacles placed across a prominent Roman nose, black kerchief arranged with no great attention to precision, and, to complete the picture, a little black rattan flourished in his hand. His bearing as he walked was tolerably upright and marked with that indescribable swing, always assumed by those who pride themselves on being good pedestrians. As a musician, he was greater than Bach, as a poet he surpassed Byron, as a painter, Claude Loraine, as a rebel he snatched the Palm from Alexander Rogue, as a merchant, Edward Percey was his inferior, as mill-owner, Granville came not near him, as a traveller, De Humboldt, Ledyard, Mungo Park, etc., never braved half his dangers or overcame half his difficulties.

Branwell, from the pinnacle of his self-importance, viewed his sisters with patronizing derision. Charlotte, in another tale, whose hero is obviously Branwell, writes that:

When he was asked whether his sisters were as "queer as he," he replied, "Oh, they are miserable, silly creatures, not worth talking about. C's eighteen years old, a broad, dumpy thing, whose head does not come higher than my elbow. E's lean and scant, with a face about the size of a penny, and A is nothing, absolutely nothing."

"What is she, an idiot?"

"Next door to it," he replied.

And when the Branwell prototype is asked the reason for his desire to leave Haworth, which he describes as, "a miserable little village buried in dreary moors and bogs and marshes," he replies that he is "not satisfied with being a sign painter in the village as them things were with being semptresses."

In the minds of the Brontes, Branwell was headed almost inevitably for artistic distinction.

When Miss Nussey visited Haworth, and Branwell was aged sixteen, the Brontes already foresaw him as a great artist. Miss Nussey writes:

> Branwell, already painting in oils, which was regarded as study for what might eventually be his future profession. All the household entertained the idea of his becoming an artist and hoped that he would be a distinguished one.

Yet the truth was that he was probably singularly unqualified. Branwell's later friend, the noted Halifax sculptor, J. Leyland, the only professional artist among Branwell's intimates, stated that as a painter Branwell had only a "moderate talent."

Mr. Bronte "greatly admired the Arts. They afford me peculiar pleasure," as he wrote to his children's drawing teacher, William Robinson. But, preoccupied by his ministerial duties in Haworth, Mr. Bronte probably had no real knowledge of the talent and technical training necessary for a professional artistic career. Certainly Mr. Bronte did not dissuade his son from the latter's various abortive attempts in his career as a painter. Mr. Bronte paid for Branwell's artistic fiascos.

When, at eighteen, he took the initial step in his artistic career, his attempt to enter the Royal Academy in London, Branwell's only qualifications seem to have been the Bronte dream of artistic renown; a minutely drawn map of London; sparse training, some talent and extremely self-indulgent habits. Almost inevitably, Branwell failed tragically. In London, Branwell, like the traditional "artist-manque" burdened with unrealistic, high expectations, ended, as Branwell wrote of a hero in one of his own tales, by "fortifying himself with little squibs of rum." But even more fatally, Branwell's first failure set a precedent of evasive experience which Branwell repeated in later life.

The details of Branwell's trip to London remain vague. He probably reached London during the late summer or early fall of 1835. Early that spring, Branwell wrote to the secretary of the Royal Academy requesting permission to submit his drawings—a prerequisite to entering the Academy—in July or August. And Mr. Bronte, in writing to Branwell's drawing teacher, Mr. Robinson, in July, had stated: "It is my design to enroll my son in The Royal Academy."

But Branwell's few months in London are obscured in a mist of tavern-crawling, unpaid tavern debts, a close friendship with a well-known prize fighter, and roaming the city streets. Apparently Branwell visited some historical landmarks. He later did a drawing of Westminster Abbey from memory. But he made his *real* headquarters in London at a famous sporting bar, The Castle Tavern, Holborn. He probably never presented himself at the Royal Academy. In his Angrian tale, "Charles Wentworth's Visit to Verdepolis," Branwell is obviously describing his London experiences. The tale's Branwell-like hero travels to a great city, but fearing to endanger his dream of himself as a great artist, does not present his letters of introduction to the art gallery directors. The reason, according to Branwell, was due to his hero's "instinctive fear of ending his pleasure by approaching reality."

Branwell returned to Haworth during the late autumn, debt-ridden and disillusioned.

Emily's disillusionment with her brother probably became more definite after his London fiasco. Emily was, perhaps, the most romantically idealistic of the three sisters, as she reveals in her poetry. Emily, like Charlotte and Anne, had *high* moral principles. As Ellen Nussey once wrote, the sisters were "on common ground if a principle had to be maintained or a shame detected." Emily's feelings about Branwell's behavior —his drunkenness, his debts, his failures—are easily imagined.

Yet Emily, as her poems prove, deeply loved Branwell. Thus, Emily's feelings about Branwell were a source of anguished, inner conflict. During her twenties, she wrote many poems, which describe mixed emotions; love and hate, admiration and scorn for the same person, a sinner, inspired by Branwell, in an attempt to heal and solve her emotional ambivalence.

Indeed, it seems to this writer that much of Emily's great writing, including *Wuthering Heights* was to be fired by her unhappy, inner conflict about Branwell.

5

EMILY AND CHARLOTTE IN ROE HEAD

W<small>HILE</small> B<small>RANWELL</small> was meeting misfortune in London, Emily had a harsher and perhaps, from her viewpoint, more distasteful reality to meet. The demands on Mr. Bronte's limited income were rapidly mounting. Branwell's London trip during this summer of (1835) would be a heavy expense. Emily needed to prepare to earn her living either as a private governess or a teacher, the only two possible professions for poor gentlewomen. Emily must do like Charlotte who, according to Miss Nussey, had entered Roe Head School to "Fit herself for governess life." Charlotte now arranged with her former headmistress, Miss Wooler, to pay Emily's tuition in Roe Head, by teaching there. Charlotte accepted the incredibly tiny salary of sixteen pounds (about $80.00) a year, which included Emily's clothes as well as her own.

Although Charlotte felt deeply that it was her duty to support herself, she obviously detested the idea of becoming a teacher. As she wrote to Ellen, on July 6th, 1835, expressing both her reluctance to leave Haworth and her dread of "entering a situation"—"better sune as syne," quoting an old Scotch proverb. Charlotte's distaste was somewhat softened because, as Charlotte wrote, she "both loved and respected" Miss Wooler.

Emily and Charlotte planned to leave Haworth for Roe Head on July 29th, 1835. The move was apparently dreaded also by Emily. As Charlotte explained to Ellen: "The idea of being to-gether consoles us somewhat."

In Emily's and Charlotte's momentous undertaking Mr. Bronte, with almost Victorian parental fear for the moral well-being of his two nearly adult daughters, entrusted them to the friendly if rather distant care of his Thornton friend, Miss Firth, now Mrs. Franks of Huddersfield. He writes on July 6, 1835:

> As two of my dear children are to be placed near you, I take the liberty to request you and Mr. Franks to be so kind as to interpose with your advice and counsel to them in case of necessity, and, if expedient to write to Miss Branwell or me if our interference should be requisite. I will charge them to attend strictly to what you advise. They both have good abilities, and as far as I can judge, their principles are good also, but they are very young and unacquainted with the ways of this delusive and insnaring world . . . neither they nor any other can ever, in this land of probation, lie beyond the reach of temptation.

For Emily, the experience was doomed to fail. Abruptly transplanted to an unfamiliar environment; forced to adhere to a daily routine among people to whom, perhaps, because of dissimilar interests and her own reserve she was indifferent; feeling imprisoned by the rigid discipline—she ailed psychically, morally, and even physically. Charlotte noticed Emily's increasing melancholia and after three months, fearing that if Emily's ordeal were prolonged Emily might really die, mercifully arranged for Anne to replace Emily. In her biographical notes on her sisters, Charlotte movingly described Emily's depression at Roe Head:

> My sister Emily loved the moors. Flowers brighter than the rose bloomed in the blackest heath for her; out of a sullen hollow in a livid hillside, her mind could make an Eden. She found in the bleak solitude many and dear delights; and not the least and best-loved was liberty. Liberty

was the breath of Emily's nostrils; without it she perished.
The change from her own home to a school, and from her
own very noiseless, very secluded, but unrestricted and un-
artificial mode of life to one of disciplined routine (though
under the kindest auspices) was what she failed in enduring.
Her nature was here too strong for her fortitude. Every
morning when she woke the visions of home and the moors
rushed on her, and darkened and saddened the day that lay
before her. Nobody knew what ailed her but me. I knew
only too well. In this struggle, her health was quickly
broken; her white face, attenuated form, and failing
strength threatened rapid decline. I felt in my heart she
would die if she did not go home.

But Miss Nussey, writing years later to Mrs. Gaskell, described Emily's dejection in more homely terms, "She never
settled and was ill from nothing but homesickness. Anne took
her place and remained about two years."

When Emily left Roe Head in the early autumn, nothing
indicates that she regretted leaving either Roe Head itself or
any person, pupil, or teacher. Neither Emily's poems nor her
diaries, nor Charlotte's references to Emily, suggest that
Emily had experienced even the shadow of a personal tie
Her isolation, emotionally, was unequivocal.

Charlotte endured her ordeal as a teacher for another two
and a half years until late spring, 1838. She developed a different type but barely less severely crippling neurasthenic illness than Emily's. Essentially, Charlotte's psychological difficulty prevailed with varying degrees of intensity until she
became a successful novelist, permanently freed from the
drudgery of earning a living in a profession which she deeply
resented. Her mental disquiet was caused by an almost lifelong and nearly unendurable inner conflict between her sense
of duty (in Roe Head her dreary teaching duties) and her
latent, inward dream of being a novelist. Charlotte's physical

health was to repeatedly break down under the terrible strain. Charlotte's problems affected Emily profoundly by helping create the atmosphere of despair and defeat at the parsonage, which Emily accepted as an inescapable part of life in Haworth—a fact which Emily makes clear in many of her later poems.

In Roe Head, for example, Charlotte, more mindful than Emily of Aunt Branwell's morbid, Methodist strictures (in Charlotte's words, "A's ghastly Calvinist doctrines"), fell into a religious melancholia, rooted in her internal dilemma. She bitterly reproached herself for being unreasonably discontented; for her arrogant, unChristian detestation of both her work and her pupils; for self-indulgently pursuing her own sheerly selfish dreams instead of the tenets of her religion and her patent duty. She began to feel obsessively guilt-ridden, and viewed herself as an unredeemable sinner.

To Ellen she writes:

> If you knew my thoughts; the dreams that absorb me and the fiery imaginations that at times eat me up and make me feel Society as it *is*, wretchedly insipid, you would pity me and I dare say despise me.

And in her Roe Head diary:

> I fulfill my duties strictly and well—but as God was not in the fire, nor the wind, nor the earthquake, so neither is my heart in my task, the theme, or the exercise. It is the still, small voice always that comes to me at Eventide, that takes up my spirit and engrosses all my living feelings, all my energies which are not merely mechanical.

And again to Ellen:

> I keep trying to do right, checking wrong feelings, repressing wrong thoughts. But, still, I feel myself going astray. I have a constant tendency to scorn people who are

better than I am . . . a dread lest, if I made the slightest profession, I should sink into Pharaseeism, merge wholly into the ranks of the self-righteous.

And, in another letter to Ellen:

I know not how to pray; I cannot bend my life to the grand end of doing good. I go on constantly seeking my own pleasure, pursuing the gratification of my own desires. I forget God, and will not God forget me?

In her abject self-loathing, Charlotte despaired of salvation, fearing that she was eternally doomed:

I abhor myself . . . I despise myself, if the doctrines of Calvin be true, I am already an outcast. You cannot imagine how hard, rebellious and intractable all my feelings are. When I begin to study on the subject, I almost grow blasphemous, atheistical in my sentiment . . .

. . . a longing for holiness which I shall never, never attain . . . darkened, in short, by the very shadows of Spiritual Death. If Christian perfection is necessary to Salvation, I shall never be saved. My head is a real hot-bed for sinful thoughts, and as to practise, when I decide on any action, I scarcely remember to look to my Redeemer for direction.

To Charlotte, Ellen seemed very nearly a saint. Charlotte envisions Ellen, from the depths of her own self-hatred:

It is from religion that you derived your chief charm, and may its influence always preserve you as pure, as unassuming, and as benevolent in thought and deed as you are now. What am I compared to you? I feel my own worthlessness when I make the comparison. I am a very coarse, commonplace wretch, Ellen. I have some qualities which make me very miserable . . . I don't pride myself on these peculiarities. I strive to conceal and suppress them as much as I can, but they burst out sometimes, and those who see the explosion despise me and I hate myself for days afterwards.

And:

Don't deceive yourself by imagining that I have a bit of real goodness about me. My darling, if I were like you . . . *but I am not like you.*

In her extremity, as her distress became more acute, she even visualized retiring to a rustic retreat with Ellen. And her emotional dependence on Ellen has a temporarily homosexual tinge. She writes that in a humble hut she and Ellen could read the Bible and devote themselves to spiritual self-improvement:

If we had a cottage of our own . . . I do think we might live and love TILL DEATH . . . If I could always live with you and daily read the Bible with you, if your lips and mine could at the same time drink the same draught from the same pure fountain of mercy, I hope, I might one day become better than my evil wandering thoughts, my corrupt heart, cold to the spirit and warm to the flesh, will now permit me to be.

Thus, in Roe Head, Charlotte, burdened by a tiring teaching schedule, was also inwardly racked by night by self-doubt.

Yet Emily's more purely inward battles were, in the perspective of their entire lives, perhaps more complex and insurmountable.

6

EMILY—

A POET AND TEACHER

ALTHOUGH CHARLOTTE claimed that: "It was some years before the experiment of sending her from home was again ventured on," Emily left Haworth in the early autumn of 1837 to teach at Miss Patchett's School, Law Hill House, Southwarum, near Halifax.

Miss Patchett's, somewhat larger than Roe Head, was a semi-fashionable finishing school for Halifax young ladies. But Southwarum, like Haworth, was a grey stone town, set high among moorland hills on the edge of a vast moorland range—Oxenhope Moor. Four miles below the town, over a steep mountain road, was the industrial town of Halifax.

Emily's meagrely recorded tenure here apparently resembled her experience at Roe Head. But, as a teacher, Emily had a gruelling work routine. Charlotte, writing on October 2, 1837, to Ellen, states:

> My sister, Emily, has gone into a situation as a teacher in a large school near Halifax of nearly forty pupils. I have had one letter since her departure. It gives an appalling account of her duties—hard labour from six in the morning until near eleven at night, with only one half hour of exercise between. This is slavery . . . Emily will never stand it.

But apparently Emily endured it for at least six months. The actual length of time remains vague. But Emily probably remained at Miss Patchett's until the (1838-9) Christmas holidays. She wrote several poems describing her nostalgia for Haworth and her unhappy exile, during the Autumn of 1838.

Emily evidently found a refuge from and a compensation for bleak, dreary drudgery in this school, which had little to give her beyond some background for *Wuthering Heights* (Law Hill House had a *Wuthering Heights*-like history of revenge), in writing poetry. Her passion for her native moors, fired by denial and by the mood of prison-like gloom, which according to Charlotte, obsessed Emily whenever she felt unnaturally hemmed in, stimulated Emily to write some of her finest nature poems, which foreshadow her mature poetry.

Until now, Emily, unlike Charlotte and Branwell, who had sent poems to Wordsworth and Southey (the poet laureate), had been tentative and uncertainly fearful about her poetry. In despair, Emily had written the lines in August, 1837, about a month before arriving at Miss Patchett's:

> I ask myself, "O why has heaven
> Denied the precious gift to me,
> The glorious gift to many given
> To speak their thoughts in poetry?
>
> Dreams have encircled me," I said,
> From careless childhood's sunny time;
> Visions by ardent fancy fed
> Since life was in its morning prime.
>
> But now, when I had hoped to sing,
> My fingers strike a tuneless string;
> And still the burden of the strain
> Is "Strive no more; 'tis all in vain."

And, as Emily had noted beneath her very first poem,

I am more terrifically and idiotically and brutally STUPID than I ever was in the whole course of my existence. The above precious lines are the fruits of one hour's most agonizing labour between half past six and half past seven in the evening of July '36.

But at Miss Patchett's, Emily's exile fired her, in poems which reveal the depth of her boredom and frustration here, to write movingly about her native moors. On November 11, 1838, Emily writes:

> What language can utter the feeling
> That rose when, in exile, afar,
> On the brow of a lonely hill kneeling
> I saw the brown heath growing there.
>
> Well, well, the sad minutes are moving
> Though loaded with trouble and pain;
> And sometime the loved and the loving
> Shall meet on the mountains again.

And, in December, 1838, in one of her most famous poems, appear the lines:

> A little while, a little while
> The noisy crowd are barred away;
> And I can sing and I can smile
> A little while I've holyday!
>
> Where wilt thou go, my harassed heart?
> Full many a land invites thee now;
> And places near and far apart
> Have rest for thee, my weary brow.
>
> There is a spot 'mid barren hills,
> Where winter howls and driving rain;
> But if the tempest chills
> There is a light that warms again.
>
> The house is old, the trees are bare,
> And moonless bends the misty dome;
> But what on earth is half so dear,
> So longed for as the hearth of home?

A little and a lone green lane,
That opened on a common wide;
A distant, dreamy, blue chain,
Of mountains circling every side;

A heaven so clear, an earth so calm,
So sweet, so soft, so hushed an air;
And, deepening still the dream-like charm,
Wild moor-sheep feeding everywhere—

Even as I stood with raptured eye,
Absorbed in bliss so deep and dear;
My hour of rest had fleeted by,
And given me back to weary care.

And in her poem of December 18, 1838, the stanza:

How do I yearn, how do I pine
For the time of flowers to come,
And turn me from that fading shine
To mourn the fields of home.

And, here, Emily began to explore her inner lifelong torment about Branwell. Emily's close and yet anguished relationship with her brother had evidently reached a climactic phase in the few years before Emily had left Haworth for Miss Patchett's.

Difficult as it is to identify Emily's love or loves in her poems (or even if real or imaginary, or sexually fulfilled or not) yet the few known facts about her personal life, combined with a careful reading of *Wuthering Heights* and her love poems, do reveal a definite emotional pattern. The latter can be linked, however tenuously, to her own experiences. Many of Emily's love poems, written at Miss Patchett's, describe mixed emotions about a beloved sinner. Branwell's pattern of tragic experiences had recently emerged.

Emily's love, in some of these poems, is not a new love. As she writes in October, 1837:

> But that pure light, changeless and strong,
> Cherished and watched and nursed so long;
> That love that first its glory gave
> Shall be my pole star to the grave.

And,

> Now trust a heart that trusts in you,
> And firmly say the word "Adieu";
> Be sure, wherever I may roam,
> My heart is with your heart at home;

And, in another poem, December 14, 1837, appears the stanza:

> Down on the skirts of Areon's forest
> There lies a lone and lovely glade;
> And there the hearts together nourished
> Their first, their fatal parting made.

Certainly Emily is referring to Branwell? Varied phases of the same tragic theme constantly recur: a broken inner dream about a loved one, a disillusionment in love, an irrevocable parting. Emily and Branwell had recently been twice tragically parted: the first time (in 1835), when Branwell went to London and Emily to Roe Head, and the second, when Emily went to Miss Patchett's.

Thus, Emily writes, on August 19, 1837, perhaps remembering Branwell's departure for London:

> O Alexander! When I return
> Warm as those hearths my heart would burn
> Light as thine own, my foot would fall
> If I might hear thy voice in the hall.

> But thou art now on a desolate sea—
> Parted from Gondal and parted from me—
> All my repining is hopeless and vain,
> Death never yields back its victims again.

And, again in December, 1837, appear the lines:

> Ten years ago in last September
> Fernando left his home and you,
> And still I think you must remember
> The anguish of that last adieu;
>
> And well you know how, wildly pining,
> I longed to see his face again
> Through all the Autumn's drear declining,
> Its stormy nights and days of rain.
>
> And there I stood, when he had left me,
> With ashy cheek and tearless eye,
> Watching the ship whose sail bereft me
> Of life and hope and peace and joy.
>
> It past; that night I sought a pillow
> Of sleepless woe, and grieving lone
> My soul still hovered o'er the billow,
> And mourned a love forever flown.
>
> Yet smiling bright in recollection,
> One blissful hour returns to me:
> One letter told of firm affection,
> Of safe deliverance from the sea;
>
> But not another. Fearing, hoping,
> Spring, winter, harvest, glided o'er;
> And time at length brought power for coping
> With thoughts I could not once endure.

And, in a poem in February, 1838, which is another variation of the tragic-parting theme:

> Weaned from life and torn away
> In the morning of thy day;
> Bound in everlasting gloom;
> Buried in a hopeless tomb;
>
> Yet upon thy bended knee
> Thank the power (that) banished thee;

Chain and bar and dungeon wall
Saved them from a deadlier thrall.

Thank the power that made thee part
Ere that parting broke thy heart.

Finally, Emily's two poems, written in the springs of 1838 and 1839, which, along with a few later poems have given rise to the theory that Emily and Branwell had incestuous relations. Her poem dated May 9th, 1838, reads in part:

Why do I hate that lone green dell?
Buried in moors and mountain wild,
That is a spot I had loved too well
Had I but seen it when a child.

There are bones whitening there in the summer's heat,
But it is not for that, and none can tell;
None but one can the secret repeat
Why I hate that lone green dell.

Noble foe, I pardon thee
All thy cold and scornful pride,
For thou wast a priceless friend to me
When my sad heart had none beside.

And leaning on thy generous arm,
A breath of old times over me came;
The earth shone round with long-lost charm;
Alas, I forgot I was not the same.

And, a poem, on March 27, 1839, also hints at a hidden crime:

What winter floods, what showers of spring
Have drenched the grass by night and day;
And yet, beneath, the spectre ring,
Unmoved and undiscovered lay.

A mute remembrancer of crime,
Long lost, concealed, forgot for years,
It comes at last to cancel time,
And waken unavailing tears.

But incest is a mere theory. For though Emily describes an early sin, in neither poem is there a direct link to Branwell beyond the general love-crime motif.

But, whatever the nature of Emily's and Branwell's love, certainly one of Emily's poetic love-themes (Emily may also have experienced a homosexual love, here, as some biographers have suggested) was rooted in Branwell. It seems to this writer that Emily and Branwell's love resembled the quasi-romantic, over-intense, Heathcliff-Cathy type early love, when in *Wuthering Heights* they had roamed the moors, bound by blood-like ties (Emily very carefully makes Heathcliff Cathy's foster brother), a passion for nature and early dreams. A few lines in a later poem (dated January, 1841 and May, 1844) are almost conclusive proof:

> Listen; I've known a burning heart
> To which my own was given;
> Nay, not in passion; do not start—
> Our love was love from heaven;
> At least, if heavenly love be born
> In the pure light of childhood's morn—
> Long ere the poison-tainted air
> From this world's plague-fen rises here.

Emily's pattern of emotional ambiguity toward Branwell, which motivated many of her best poems and finally *Wuthering Heights*, had begun.

7

CHARLOTTE AND BRANWELL:
EMERGING PATTERNS

W<small>HEN</small> E<small>MILY</small> returned to Haworth from her self-described imprisonment at Miss Patchett's (probably during
the 1838-39 Christmas holidays), Charlotte and Branwell
were moving toward the central crises and dilemmas in their
lives. Emily, herself unnaturally mature in certain respects,
was personally resigned. She had developed, in the words of
her poem, a "Courage to endure" philosophy. But the deep,
lifelong frustrations of the other Brontes instilled in Emily
a tragic feeling of despair and defeatism from which there
seemed to be no escape. One remembers her lines written on
May 25th, 1839:

> If heaven would rain on me
> That future storm of care,
> So their fond hearts were free
> I'd be content to bear.
>
> But the glad eyes around me
> Must weep as mine have done
> And I must see the same gloom
> Eclipse their morning sun.

Charlotte's and Branwell's difficult problems seemed nearly
insoluble. Charlotte's and Branwell's twenties were especially
agonizing. Their inner conflicts between the need to earn
a living (which weighed more heavily on Mr. Bronte's eldest,
most able daughter and his son, than on Emily and Anne) and

the contrary drive to fulfill their artistic dreams was self-defeating. It was an admittedly vital factor in Branwell's tragedy and in Charlotte's various breakdowns.

Perhaps more consciously than one realizes with our familiar mental picture of the Brontes as naturally gifted writers, they were all almost fanatically—and poignantly—determined to realize, as Charlotte once wrote: "The early dream of one day becoming authors."

But neither Charlotte nor Branwell nor Anne, nor of course, Emily had yet managed to emerge from their private childhood, fantasy-tale writing to become adult writers. To Emily's eldest sister and her brother, the tangible rewards of literary achievement were a particularly compelling and definite goal. Charlotte and Branwell now made various abortive attempts at publication. And Charlotte and Branwell were also faced with the more distressing problem—the need to make a living in a remote backwater.

Since his London fiasco, Branwell dilettantishly alternated painting, in his second-floor, homemade parsonage studio, with writing and an occasional, temporary job. Increasingly addicted to alcohol and tavern debts, in Charlotte's phrase, "He settled to nothing."

Branwell had recently joined a Masonic Lodge, The Three Graces, whose headquarters were, unfortunately, The Black Bull Inn. As the lodge's secretary, junior warden and organist, Branwell was often at The Black Bull. And he met the local Bohemians in the nearby Keighley and Bradford Inns. During the (1838-39) winter when Emily was in Southwarum (and Branwell's expenses may have been a reason why Emily continued teaching), he had made a second, ill-fated attempt to translate his artistic dreams into reality. In a Bradford studio, paid for by Mr. Bronte, Branwell tried to establish himself as a portrait painter. But though his friend, Francis Grundy, claimed that Branwell achieved considerable success, he ended disastrously. Isolated, doubtless lonely, and poor, Branwell dissipated time and energy and money in meeting the intelligentsia at the local Inns: the George Hotel and the Bull's Head Tavern. The local artists, a distinguished group, included John James, the historian; Wilson Anderson, the painter; Richard Waller, a portrait painter, and occasionally, J. Leyland, the Halifax sculptor, Branwell's lifelong friend. Finally, Mr. Bronte wisely recalled him to Haworth during the spring. Branwell, psychically and physically disintegrated, returned to the parsonage, leaving his studio rent unpaid and an unfinished portrait in Bradford. He had painted only a very few portraits.

Branwell's second artistic defeat probably led to his drug addiction. For, shortly after his return to Haworth, during a brief recuperative trip to Liverpool with his friend, John Brown, he probably took his first dose of opium.

Branwell, weak and imitative, and a passionate admirer of De Quincey and Coleridge, now emulated these poets. F. Grundy, in explaining Branwell's drug taking, stated, "He had been studying De Quincey and with the obstinate determination of doing himself whatever anyone else had done, he began the practice of opium-eating."

Branwell was again at a dead-end.

Charlotte, since her return from her teaching job, was almost equally rudderless. Her teaching career had, at least temporarily, ended. But Charlotte was far more ironly determined. Charlotte, unlike Branwell, had a more clear-sighted understanding of and ability to deal with, in her own words, "stern necessity." Indeed, she had a Protestant reverence for, in Shakespeare's phrase, "the uses of adversity." As she wrote during her forthcoming ordeal as a private governess, "Adversity is a good school—the Poor are born to labor, the Dependent to endure—the ordeal would do me good, I reflected."

Eventually, Charlotte was, of course, undefeated. But, if finally victorious, she was permanently psychically maimed, as those who knew her during her celebrity testified. Much of her original spirit had been diluted. Not even her literary renown entirely revived it. Even when she became one of the most widely read women novelists in England, an underlying melancholy remained, as her own letters and Mrs. Gaskell's personal impression of Charlotte attest.

Both Charlotte and Branwell, in turning from writing about their fantasy Angrian world (begun in 1829) to more adult writing, had met repeated defeat. Branwell, since the age of seventeen, had bombarded *Blackwood's* with his dramatic, even threatening pleadings. By December, 1835, he had already written *Blackwood's* at least three times, literally begging to be published. His letters are sadly revealing of his unhappy, confused, unbalanced mentality. They read less like letters to another person than like private self-analyses of elements within himself, which he, Branwell, did not understand.

In one of these early letters Branwell writes, "The idea of my striving to aid another periodical is *horribly* repulsive. . . . You have lost an able writer in James Hogg and God grant that you may gain one in Patrick Branwell Bronte."

And, in a letter dated April, 1836, enclosing a poem, "Misery," Branwell writes:

> Not to think, Sir, that I write nothing but MISERIES. My day is far too much in the morning for such continued shadow. Nor think either (and this I entreat) that I wish to deluge you with poetry. I send it because it is soonest read and comes from the heart—if it goes to yours print it and write me on the subject of *contribution*. Then I will send you prose. But if what I now write is worthless, what I have said is only conceit and folly—*yet condemn not unheard.*

But *Blackwood's* remained silent. Branwell, enraged, demanded a personal interview:

I hinted that I was in possession the design (of which) would be far superior to any series which has yet appeared in Blackwoods. But a description by letter (is) quite impossible. Surely a journey of three hundred miles shall not deter me . . . all I ask you is to permit this interview . . . Will you so wearisomely refuse me a word . . . Do you think your magazine so perfect that no addition would be either possible or desirable? Is it pride that actuates you— or custom—or prejudice. Be a man, Sir! and think no more of these things. *Write* to me.

Blackwood's still was silent.

During Charlotte's Christmas (1836-37) holidays in Haworth, she and Branwell had decided to write, respectively, to Southey and Wordsworth for literary advice. Each had enclosed verses. Charlotte's letter to Southey has not been preserved. But, on January 19th, 1837, Branwell wrote to Wordsworth. Branwell's letter, again, a self-analytic essay, is a strange mixture of a perhaps compulsive defense of the purity of his motives and ideals in literature, self-glorification; monetary fears; hidden threats and obvious flattery. He writes:

I most earnestly entreat you to read and pass judgment . . . from my birth to my nineteenth year, I have lived among secluded hills, where I could neither know what I was or what I could do. I read for the same reason that I ate or drank—it was a real craving of nature. I wrote out of the impulses and feelings of the mind. And, not, from self-conceit that could not receive food from flattery, since not half a dozen people know that I ever penned a line. But, now, . . . I must do something for myself; the powers I possess must be exercised to a definite end, and as I don't know, myself, I must ask others what they are worth.

And, of Wordsworth's own writings, he continued, "One whose works I have most loved in our literature . . . a divinity of the mind from whose sentence there is no appeal, who may claim a place in the memory for a thousand years to come." And, again, referring to his personal ideals, "I trust not poetry alone; that might launch the vessel, but could not bear her on, sensible and scientific prose, bold and vigorous efforts . . . would give further notice (by) the world"; and, "Poetry ought to brighten and crown that name with glory." "Surely, when there is not a poet writing worth sixpence, the field must be open, if a better man can step forward."

Branwell included a brief outline of his enclosed work, in which, interestingly enough, he predicted his own destiny!

> The Prefatory scene in which I have developed strong passions and weak principles struggling with a high imagination and acute feelings, till, as youth hardens into age, evil deeds and enjoyments end in mental and bodily ruin . . . return me an answer, telling me whether I should write or write no more.

Reputedly, Wordsworth was repelled. He did not reply. According to Southey (in a letter to a friend), "Wordsworth was disgusted with the letter for it contained gross flattery and plenty of abuse of other poets."

Charlotte finally received a belated reply from Southey in March, 1837. It was only barely more encouraging than Wordsworth's silence. Southey, who felt, as he wrote a friend, that "The poor girl's letter was flighty," wrote her a "Cooling dose of admonition." Though the poet recognized that Charlotte had a degree of talent, with the caution of the elderly renowned he tried to deflect her from a career which he believed not only unwise but psychologically dangerous for a woman. As he gravely forewarned her:

You evidently possess what Wordsworth calls the faculty of verse . . . in these times it is not rare. But I feel bound in duty, to caution against so perilous a course. The day dreams in which you indulge induce a distempered state of mind . . . and, as the ordinary uses of the world seem flat and unprofitable, you will be unfitted for them without becoming fitted for anything else. Literature cannot be the business of a woman's life, and it ought not to be. Nevertheless, write poetry for its own sake, and not with a view to celebrity.

Charlotte, reasonably, tried to benefit from discouragement. On March 16th, 1837, she had replied from Roe Head:

. . . the kind and wise advice. At first perusal of your letter, I felt only shame and regret that I had troubled you with my crude rhapsody. But after I had read it again and again . . . You do not say that what I write is utterly destitute of merit. You warn me against neglecting real duties for imaginative pleasures.

And denying that she is an "idle, dreaming being," she adds:

I fulfilled my duty when I left school to become a governess. But in the evenings, I do think . . . but . . . I avoid any appearance of eccentricity and preoccupation. I observe all the duties a woman ought to fulfill, but when I'm teaching or sewing I would rather be reading or writing. But I try to deny myself. I trust I shall never more feel ambitious to see my name in print. If the wish should rise, I shall look at your letter and suppress it. Your advice shall not be wasted, however sorrowfully and reluctantly.

In a few days (March 22nd, 1837) Southey replied, slightly less severely:

You have received admonition kindly. Let me request,

if you ever come to these Lakes, let me see you. You would then think of me with more good will; you would then perceive there is neither severity nor moroseness in my state of mind. I hope you will keep a quiet mind; for your moral and spiritual improvement will then keep pace with your intellectual powers.

Charlotte did remember Southey kindly. Rather touchingly, she wrote on the cover of Southey's letter, "Southey's advice. To be kept forever."

But Charlotte, indomitable, within two years made her first attempt at writing a realistic novel. Evidently, Charlotte was not yet capable of bridging the transition from the lush, romantic, melodramatic Angrian tales to realism.

Wordsworth, to whom Charlotte sent part of her novel in 1840, evidently thought it melodramatic and pseudo-Richardsonian. Replying to the poet's critique, she agreed that:

No doubt if I had gone on, I should have made quite a Richardsonian concern of it . . . I am sorry I did not exist fifty or sixty years ago when the Ladies' Magazine was flourishing. In that case my aspirations after literary fame would have met with due encouragement. I recollect getting hold of some antiquated volumes and reading them by stealth and the most exquisite pleasure.

Not permanently defeated, she renounced her first novel, however. As she wrote Wordsworth, "I can give it up without much distress."

Charlotte's present, ill-fated trials as a novelist continued until about a year before Emily died—when *Jane Eyre* was finally published in 1847. Branwell's artistic failures, except for his publication of an occasional poem in a local paper and the praise of friends (including Coleridge's son, Hartley, who admired Branwell's translation of an Ode of Horace), ended only with his death. In a word, Charlotte's and Branwell's defeats were a permanent part of the pattern of Emily's life at the parsonage.

8

EMILY AT HAWORTH PARSONAGE

Although the detailed background of Emily's personal relations to Branwell, as his outrages accumulated, is vague, his moral collapse was her major preoccupation immediately after her return from Miss Patchett's.

Indeed, both because of her circumstances and her temperament, there was little means of escape. In the frustrating atmosphere of the parsonage, Emily was more or less permanently bound. Nothing occurred in Emily's life, except for some months in a Brussels school, a few years hence, to disrupt her emotional roots in Haworth.

Now she became even more deeply inured at the parsonage. With the departure of Taby (due to lameness following a leg-accident), and presently of Charlotte and Anne, Emily became the parsonage housekeeper. The Brontes had retired the incapacitated Taby, temporarily, to live with her sister in Haworth. But since they had an almost morbid passion for privacy and aversion to strangers and a lingeringly childlike devotion for this aging foster-mother-servant, they decided not to replace her.

Charlotte explained the reasons why they had chosen drudgery, to Ellen in December, 1839:

> Emily and I are sufficiently busy—I manage the ironing and keep the rooms clean. Emily does the baking and attends to the kitchen. We are such odd animals that we prefer this mode of contrivance to having a new face

amongst us. But we do not despair of Taby's return, and she shall not be supplanted by a stranger in her absence.

And she added, in amused self-derision: "I excited Aunt's wrath very much by burning the clothes the first time I attempted to iron." And, then pointing out a trait even truer of Emily:

> Human feelings are queer things. I am much happier black-leading stoves, making beds, and sweeping floors, at home, than I should be living like a fine lady anywhere else.

But if Emily preferred domestic tasks to entering "a situation," in Charlotte's words, in Haworth, Emily was particularly isolated. Charlotte, when in Haworth, not only taught a Sunday School class, but she was absorbed in the lives of the local curates, whom both she and her friend, Ellen, viewed as prospective husbands. And she was engaged in her various plans to get teaching and governessing jobs. Also she actively maintained, if mostly by letter, various relationships, including her two Roe Head friendships with Miss Taylor and Miss Nussey.

Branwell had a variety of activities and interests. He both practised the three Arts at home and he had a number of neighborhood friends whom he met at the Black Bull and other local inns.

But Emily, especially when alone in Haworth, was literally spiritually marooned. And only Emily, from this spring (1839), remained uninterruptedly at the parsonage. In April, Charlotte became a private governess for a few months. And, in a second governess job, Charlotte was away from Haworth during most of the year 1841. Branwell was absent, spasmodically, in temporary jobs. Anne, from her first governess-ship, early in 1839, did not live in Haworth again until six years later, when she finally retired.

As Emily, mournful and lonely, in June, 1839, writes the
lines:

> They, they are gone! Not for a while
> As golden suns at night decline
> And even in death our grief beguile
> Foretelling, with a rose-red smile,
> How bright the morn will shine.
>
> No; these dark towers are lone and lorn;
> This very crowd is vacancy;
> And we must watch and wait and mourn
> And half look out for their return,
> And think their fair forms we see;
>
> And fancy music in our ear,
> Such as their lips could only pour;
> And think we feel their presence near,
> And start to find they are not there,
> And never shall be more!

And a few months later, in August 1839, the lines:

> Then why is all so sad and lone?
> No merry foot-step and on the stair—
> No laugh—no heart-awaking tone,
> But voiceless silence everywhere.
>
> I've wandered round our garden-ground,
> And still it seemed, at every turn,
> That I should greet approaching feet,
> And words upon the breezes borne.

Emily must have particularly missed Anne, her lifelong
Gondal collaborator. Charlotte, more frequently in Haworth,
was not, emotionally, a substitute. Emily did not have a simi-
larly deep, harmonious companionship with her elder sister,
whom in fact, she very probably resented.

Thus, Emily by temperament, as well as by her narrow
circumstances, was emotionally a particular prey to parson-

age disorders and upheavals, especially Branwell's. Fortunately, she at least utilized these creatively by attempting to resolve her agonized conflicting feelings in her poems.

Since Branwell's Bradford failure, Emily had renounced worldly if not spiritual hope for him. During the year after Emily's return from Miss Patchett's (1839), she predicted Branwell's doom, in several poems. In July, she writes the stanza:

> And blame me not, if, when the dread
> Of suffering clouds thy youthful head
> If when by crime and sorrow tost
> Thy wandering bark is wrecked and lost.

And, in September, in an even more definite poem, the stanza:

> The time is come when hope, that long
> Revived and sank, at length is o'er
> When faith in him, however strong,
> Dare prompt her to believe no more.

And in November, Emily's poem, which, though written several years before Branwell's death, is obviously a premature memorial to him:

> Well, some may hate, and some may scorn,
> And some may quite forget thy name,
> But my sad heart must ever mourn
> Thy ruined hopes, thy blighted fame.

> 'Twas thus I thought, an hour ago,
> Even weeping o'er that wretch's woe,
> One word turned back my gushing tears,
> And lit my altered eye with sneers.

> Then bless the friendly dust, I said,
> That hides thy unlamented head,
> Vain as thou wert, and weak as vain,
> The slave of falsehood, pride and pain,

My heart has nought akin to thine—
Thy soul is powerless over mine.

But these were thoughts that vanished too—
Unwise, unholy, and untrue—
Do I despise the timid deer
Because his limbs are fleet with fear?

Or would I mock the wolf's death-howl
Because his form is gaunt and foul?
Or hear with joy the leveret's cry
Because it cannot bravely die?

No! Then above his memory
Let pity's heart as tender be:
Say, "Earth lie lightly on that breast,
And, kind Heaven, grant that spirit rest!"

But, if Emily accepted, in her words, Branwell's "ruined
hopes," the moral values involved in his tragedy provided her
with a creative theme—an inner debate into the very nature
of good and evil. Emily's poems about Branwell dramatically
express conflicting emotional and mental attitudes. If he is
scorned as "weak" and "vain," etc., yet like "the timid deer"
he should not be despised. And perhaps his sins were only due
to a corrupt world? In a slightly earlier poem, she writes:

I love thee, boy; for all divine,
All full of God thy features shine.
Darling enthusiast, hold child,
Too good for this world's warring wild,
Too heavenly now but doomed to be
Hell-like in heart and misery.

And what shall change that angel brow
And quench that spirit's glorious glow?
Relentless laws that disallow
True virtue and true joy below.

And, defying Mr. Bronte's orthodox view of Sin and Damnation, she writes in March, 1840:

> Our mutual foes—they will not rest
> From trampling on thy buried breast;
> Glutting their hatred with the doom
> They picture thine, beyond the tomb.
>
> But God is not like human-kind
> Man cannot read the Almighty mind;
> Vengeance will never torture thee,
> Nor hunt thy soul eternally.
>
> Then do not in this night of grief,
> This time of overwhelming fear,
> O do not think that God can leave,
> Forget, forsake, refuse to hear!

And, again, in one of her love-for-a-sinner poems (presumably about Branwell—the only sinner known to her), in writing about his sins, his scorn, deceit, and betrayal, Emily veers between love and hate, compassion and revenge. In certain poems, the sinner is unredeemable, as in the lines written in July, 1839:

> The time of grace is past
> And mercy scorned and tried
> Forsakes to utter wrath at last
> The soul so steeled by pride.
>
> Shut from his Maker's smile
> The accursed man shall be:
> Compassion reigns a little while
> Revenge eternally.

Yet, in other poems the poet is merciful. In a poem dated May, 1840 and July, 1843, she writes:

> I know our souls are all divine;
> I know that when we die,

What seems the vilest, even like thine
A part of God himself shall shine
In perfect purity.

And, the poem's final stanza:

O could it thus forever be
That I might so adore;
I'd ask for all eternity
To make a paradise for me,
My love—and nothing more!

But this attitude is sharply contradicted in an earlier poem, in November, 1838, in the stanzas:

There, go, Deceiver, go! My hand is streaming wet;
My heart's blood flows to buy the blessing—to forget!
Oh could that lost heart give back, back again to thine,
One tenth part of the pain that clouds my dark decline!

O could I see thy lids weighed down in cheerless woe;
Too full to hide their tears, too stern to overflow;
Oh could I know thy soul with equal grief was torn;
This fate might be endured—this anguish might be borne!

Yet, this same poem ends:

And yet for all her hate, each parting glance would tell
A stronger passion breathed, burned, in this last farewell.
Unconquered in my soul the Tyrant rules me still;
LIFE bows to my control, but LOVE I cannot kill!

If Emily's love-sinner poems were obviously about Branwell, yet her own possibly guilty participation, i.e., incest, still seems to this writer, uncertain. Yet, one of these love-crime poems, if indeed Emily is writing about her relations with Branwell, is certainly extremely suggestive. (If Emily is not writing about Branwell, certainly Emily had had some other type of sexual experience?)

If I have sinned, long, long ago
That sin was purified by woe:
I've suffered on through night and day;
I've trod a dark and frightful way.

Earth's wilderness was round me spread;
Heaven's tempests beat my naked head;
I did not kneel: in vain would prayer
Have sought one gleam of mercy there:

How could I ask for pitying love,
When that grim concave frowned above,
Hoarding its lightnings to destroy
My only and my priceless joy?

They struck—and long may Eden shine
Ere I would call its glories mine:
All Heaven's undreamt felicity
Could never blot the past from me.

No; years may cloud and death may sever,
But what is done is done for ever;
And thou, false friend and treacherous guide,
Go, sate thy cruel heart with pride.

And, the later stanzas:

Thy raving, dying victim see,
Lost, cursed, degraded, all for thee!
Gaze on the wretch, recall to mind
His golden days left long behind.

Does memory sleep in Lethean rest?
Or wakes its whisper in thy breast?
O memory, wake! Let scenes return
That even her haughty heart must mourn!

Reveal, where o'er a lone green wood
The moon of summer pours,
Far down from heaven, its silver flood,
On deep Elderno's shores.

There, lingering in the wild embrace
Youth's warm affections gave,
She sits and fondly seems to trace
His features in the wave.

But, whatever Emily's personal relations with Branwell were, her inner torment about these relations and about Branwell himself is undeniable. And, actually, as is often true of unresolved conflicts in real life, Emily finally resolved it only when she dealt with it, creatively, in Art, in depicting Heathcliff's and Cathy's passion in *Wuthering Heights*, in which it flamed so magnificently.

9

EMILY, CHARLOTTE AND
ANNE: MIDDLE YEARS

Yet to Emily, Charlotte's and Anne's present disquietudes, if less dramatic and all-absorbing than Branwell's, were more deadening. In the governess careers which they now entered, Charlotte and Anne were both miserable and relative failures. Emily had a strong sense of duty, according to Miss Nussey. She felt guilty for, apparently, being idle in Haworth. Charlotte's and Anne's very tolerant defense of Emily reveals Emily's evident self-reproaches. Anne, when she noted in her diary in 1841 that "we are all doing something for our livelihood except Emily," very carefully adds, "Who, however, earns her food and raiment as much as we do." Charlotte, replying to a letter from Emily evidently filled with self-reproaches, writes to Emily from Brussels, in 1844: "You idle? Absurd, absurd."

Emily's torment was probably nevertheless real and acute. Particularly as Emily knew that governessing was deeply repugnant and temperamentally unsuitable to her sisters. Charlotte deplored the necessity of Anne's being a governess, which she believed was particularly difficult for Anne, with the latter's speech impediment and "concealed susceptibility," in Charlotte's phrase. Anne as a governess was a "patient, persecuted stranger . . . less gifted with the power of making friends than I am . . . more lonely." As Charlotte, even more forthright about her own reluctance, wrote when she took her first job: "I hate and abhor the thought of governessing."

In marriage, Charlotte might have avoided hated servitude —had she been less adamantly an individual. During this year she had refused two proposals of marriage. Miss Nussey's brother Henry, a Sussex curate, had written to propose. Charlotte had been momentarily tempted because of her emotional attachment to Ellen. As she wrote Ellen, enthusiastically, in March: "If his sister could live with me how happy I should be."

But, as she sensibly pointed out to Mr. Nussey in a piquant self-portrait: "Your wife's character should not be too marked, original; her temper should be mild . . . I am not the serious, grave, cool-headed type, but romantic, eccentric, satirical and severe."

And to Ellen: "I could not conscientiously take a grave, quiet man like Henry."

That summer, an erratic but eloquent Irish curate, named Bryce (who died shortly afterwards), after a single afternoon's meeting with Charlotte, had proposed marriage. But, characterizing him to Ellen as "witty but undignified," she had refused him.

About two months after Anne left the parsonage, Charlotte, in April, found a temporary governess job with Mrs. John Benson Sidgwick, Stonegappe, near Skipton.

Psychologically, Charlotte's and Anne's unfortunate experiences (whose repercussions reached Emily by letter) were alike. Apparently their deep resentment against the work itself was combined with an uneasy feeling of personal unfittedness. Doubtless, their discontent had a realistic basis. In an era when class distinctions were so rigid, the job of governess—a combined teacher, nursehead, household seamstress, with its vaguely menial, neither servant nor lady status—was extremely unpleasant. Charlotte's resentment was intensified by her innate dislike of children. As she wrote in complaint

of her employers' various demands, "A thing I cannot do
. . . love her children."

Charlotte, writing to Emily from Mr. Sidgwick's, in June,
described her pupils as "devils incarnate, riotous, perverse,
unmanageable cubs," and her employers (as employers invariably seemed to Charlotte) as cold and demanding. Both
Charlotte's and Anne's letters told of bitter disputes with in-
dulgent parents who refused the necessary authority to an
underling, a governess, yet demanded perfect disciplining of
their children. But Anne remained admirably patient. As
Charlotte wrote to Ellen, Anne was "eminently sensible, per-
severing in her struggle of life-wearing exertion in an unruly,
violent family of modern children" for eighteen months. Her
only mental escape was in writing an occasional Gondal or
religious poem.

Charlotte was less forbearing. After a particularly tor-
menting incident (during a gay houseparty, Mrs. Sidgwick
bitterly reproached her governess for appearing sad), she
finally admitted to Emily that she "preferred to work in a
mill."

Yet Charlotte, with admirable self-restraint, wrote to
Ellen that reflecting that "the ordeal could not last, I resolved
to be patient, to weather the storm and command my feelings." Charlotte did remain until mid-July, 1839.

A return to the parsonage was almost equally imprisoning.
The elder Bronte's rule over the sisters' lives was evidently
still fairly rigid. When Charlotte finally did return to the parsonage a trivial episode occurred, which casts an interesting
sidelight on the Elders' dominance.

While Charlotte was still in Stonegappe, Ellen had written
to suggest a two-week seaside holiday. Charlotte wrote Ellen
that "Your proposal has driven me clean daft." But transpor-
tation from Haworth to join Ellen by hired gig was expen-
sive. Charlotte wrote she was "very low in cash."

Then, unexpectedly, as she wrote to Ellen, "Aunt and Papa

determined to go to Liverpool and take us all with them." The Bronte Liverpool jaunt did not materialize.

On August 14th, when Charlotte was ready to leave Haworth, the Haworth gig was not available. Aunt Branwell and Mr. Bronte strongly disapproved of Charlotte's travelling part way by coach and thence to Ellen's on foot. Indeed, the elder Brontes became increasingly discouraging. Finally, Charlotte, dutiful and resigned, was forced to tell her friend that:

> The elders have never cordially acquiesced in the measure. Papa would willingly indulge me, but this very kindness makes me doubt whether I ought to draw on it; though I could battle Aunt's discontent, I yield to Papa. I knew he would rather I stayed at home.

Doubtless, Charlotte's holiday plans would have entirely collapsed had not Ellen unexpectedly arrived in Haworth in a borrowed carriage and literally kidnapped her friend. The two friends had then departed—in Ellen's words "almost before the horse was rested." The revolt was unprecedented. Branwell (as Ellen reported) had immediately exclaimed, "A brave defeat, the doubters were fairly taken aback."

During Charlotte's miraculous—if temporary—release, her month's seaside holiday, Charlotte experienced not only her first railroad journey but a glimpse of the sea. In Bridlington, Charlotte revealed a passion for nature as deep as Emily's. Charlotte was so profoundly moved that Ellen later recalled that when they approached the North Sea, Charlotte had speechlessly motioned to her friend to walk on ahead. She wanted to weep, undisturbed, in solitary ecstasy. Apparently she was as deeply moved as Emily was by her native moorland, to which the latter was so irrevocably bound.

Under these restrictions, it was understandable that Emily never, and Charlotte only after deep suffering, reached real maturity. Emily, in these narrow circumstances and outlook, believed that she and her sisters were doomed to be inescapably entrapped at the parsonage. Early this year (May, 1839), Emily writes the lines, certainly with her own and her sisters' lives in mind:

> Dead, dead is my joy,
> I long to be at rest;
> I wish the damp earth covered
> This desolate breast.
>
> If I were quite alone,
> It might not be so drear,
> When all hope was gone;
> At least I could not fear.
>
> Alas! as lightning withers
> The young and aged tree,
> Both they and I shall fall beneath
> The fate we cannot flee.

Emily poured her tremendous inner fire and strength increasingly into the mystic communion with Nature and Eternity which motivated much of her writing.

10

CHARLOTTE, EMILY AND ANNE
PLAN TO START
A PRIVATE SCHOOL

Emily is so silent in the Bronte annals, her rare personal remarks so restricted to purely minor events, that the real meaning to her of the few outward landmarks in her life, such as living in Brussels for some months in her twenty-fourth year, remains, like the details of her love life, hidden.

Charlotte gives various reasons for her motives in arranging for Emily and herself to enter a Brussels school. Her main motive was to learn foreign languages to prepare herself and Emily to start a private school . . . which Charlotte planned as a possible solution for the sisters' lives.

But, actually, beneath Charlotte's various rationalizations, there was a deeper motive. From Charlotte's subsequent descriptions of Emily and herself in Brussels, Emily went to Brussels, which turned out to be an irrelevant move in her own life, mainly because of Charlotte's sheerly personal desire for her own spiritual and intellectual development.

Travelling to London and Brussels meant the realization of Charlotte's early dreams. Charlotte, much more than Emily, had always romanticized great cities with their art galleries, cathedrals, and living great men. Indeed, the prospect was one of her motives in her desire for literary fame, as Mary Taylor stated in later describing Charlotte in Brussels. When, for example, her friend Ellen had visited London in 1834 and had written Charlotte, then eighteen, the latter, with the provincial naivete which she retained even during her fame, had been deeply moved. Charlotte had been astounded that Ellen had remembered her Yorkshire friend, amidst the distractions, as Charlotte had then written to Ellen:

> . . . of the great city, which to me is apocrophyl as Nineveh, ancient Rome or Babylon. I am really grateful of your mindfulness of so obscure a person as myself. Few girls would have beheld the glare, and glitter and dazzling display of London—with disposition so unchanged; hearts so uncontaminated. . .

Obviously, in Brussels Charlotte hoped to experience the delight of living in a new and wider world. For, with the touching humility which was the reverse of a certain harsh derisiveness in her nature, she frankly admitted it to Ellen. Early in November (1841) Charlotte explained to Ellen that as a result of letters from Mary Taylor who was then visiting her sister, Martha, a student in Brussels, "A fire was kindled in my heart—I longed to be something better than I am—Mary cast oil on the flames—heartened me on—I longed to go to Brussels."

But, Emily's and Charlotte's ostensible purpose in studying in Brussels was to learn languages as a background for teaching. Just then, various factors combined to decide Charlotte to head for Brussels: her dissatisfaction in a second governess job; and Mary Taylor's enthusiastic letters from Brussels.

Despite Charlotte's deep-seated aversion earlier in the year she had become a governess for a Bradford merchant—a Mr. White, Upperwood House in Rawdon, now a Leeds suburb. Charlotte had made a sacrifice in salary, because Mr. and Mrs. White had impressed even Charlotte—so often acidly critical and censorious—as "kind and worthy." As Charlotte had explained to Ellen a month after her arrival here in March, 1841:

I have made a large sacrifice in salary in the hope of securing comfort— I do not mean good eating and drinking or a warm fire, or a soft bed, but the society of cheerful faces and minds not dug out of a lead mine, or out of a marble quarry.

Inwardly Charlotte still resented a profession for which, as she rightly believed, she was singularly unqualified. She particularly hated personality adjustment; the need to be an impersonal, de-humanized, machine-like figurehead, which had proved impossible in Emily's case. She writes Ellen:

I know my place is a favorable one for a governess. What dismays and haunts me is a conviction that I have no natural knack for my vocation. If teaching were the only requisite—it would be smooth and easy; but it's living in other people's houses; the estrangement from one's real character; the adoption of a cold and frigid exterior that is painful.

While at Rawdon Charlotte, not only to free herself but also Emily and Anne from hated servitude, and yet allow them all to be together, had envisioned starting their own private school. Charlotte's idea was not entirely new. The Brontes had discussed it previously. But obtaining the necessary capital had seemed remote if not impossible.

Charlotte, now feeling increasingly entrapped, fired not only Emily's and Anne's interest but, more unexpectedly, Aunt Branwell's and Mr. Bronte's. Rather surprisingly, timidly conservative Aunt Branwell had agreed to lend the Bronte sisters about one hundred and fifty pounds from her income savings.

When Charlotte was holidaying in Haworth in July, 1841 (just missing Anne, who had returned to a new post in Thorp Green with the Reverend and Mrs. Robinson), the idea neared realization. Charlotte had tentatively fixed on East Riding which, as she told Ellen, had relatively few private schools. In mid-July, both she and Emily anxiously awaited Ellen at the parsonage, with whom they hoped to discuss the school. But when Ellen instead visited her brother in Sussex, Charlotte explained their plan by letter to Ellen on July 19th:

> We waited long and anxiously for you on Thursday. I quite wearied my eye with watching from the window, eyeglass in hand, and spectacles on the nose. But a hundred things I had to say to you will now never be said. There is a project hatching, which both Emily and I anxiously wished to discuss with you. The project is yet in its infancy, hardly peeping from its shell; and whether it will ever come out a fine full-fledged chicken, is one of those considerations but dimly revealed by the oracles of futurity.
>
> Papa and Aunt talk, by fits and starts, of our—id est, Emily, Anne and myself—commencing a school. I have often wished for such a thing, but I never could conceive where the capital was to come from. I was aware that Aunt had money, but I always considered that she was the last person who would offer a loan for the purpose. A loan she has offered, in case pupils can be secured; an eligible situation obtained, etc. But . . . I do not expect that Aunt will risk more than one hundred and fifty pounds . . . and would it be possible to establish a respectable (not by any means a showy) school with only that amount? Propound the question to your sister. As to getting into debt . . . none of us reconcile our minds to it for a moment. We do not care how modest, how humble a common cement, so it be made on sure ground . . . I have thought of Burlington or the neighborhood . . . I fancy the ground in East Riding is less fully occupied than in the West . . . And, I fear much time will elapse before any plan is executed.

Then, unexpectedly, Charlotte's former headmistress, Miss Wooler, suggested leasing Dewsbury Moor School, which had replaced Roe Head, to the Brontes, lending her furniture in return for her own room and board. Recently, the school had declined. It was now in what Charlotte termed, with perhaps an unthinking reference to the Bronte disease, "a consumptive state of health." Charlotte had immediately accepted Miss Wooler's offer, but the latter delayed her reply. In mid-summer, the Bronte school was still vague and indefinite. But Charlotte reported to Ellen, it remained the sisters' "polar star":

> No further steps have been taken nor probably will be for the present. But, Anne, Emily and I keep it in view . . . It is our polar star in all circumstances of despondency.

Did Emily really share Charlotte's enthusiasm about teaching? Emily's current diary records that Emily's true, if submerged, hopes were actually elsewhere. As Emily wrote later, "None of us has any desire for a school." In Emily's mind (much less realistic and ambitious than Charlotte's), Charlotte's proposed school existed only as a day dream. Or so she described in her "Birthday Note," July 30th, 1841, the first of two personal histories which she and Anne had agreed to write separately every four years on Emily's birthday.

Emily's tiny, enchanting vignette is embedded in between minutiae about the Brontes' pets and the Brontes' various doings and a passing reference to the characters in the Gondal Tales which she and Anne had begun writing early in the year. As in mental fantasies, a future event is often projected in the mind's eye, as already, magically, a reality—with the difficult preliminaries somehow, miraculously eliminated. Emily, in a dreamlike manner, envisages Charlotte, Anne and herself, seated in the imaginary sitting room of their already prospering school: the Brontes' debts paid—an assured idyllic future ahead. But, interestingly, Emily ends her diary on a less fanciful, austerer note. Unconsciously predicting her own future, she notes that she intends to do "great things" in writing. Emily's diary reads:

A PAPER to be opened
When Anne is
25 years old
or my next birthday after
if
all be well
Emily Jane Bronte, July 30th, 1841.

It is Friday evening, near nine o'clock—wild, rainy weather. I am seated in the dining-room, having just concluded tidying our desk boxes, writing this document. Papa is in the parlour—aunt upstairs in her room. She has been reading *Blackwood's Magazine* to Papa. Victoria and Adelaide are ensconsed in the peat-house. Keeper is in the kitchen—Hero in his cage. We are all stout and hearty, as I hope is the case with Charlotte, Branwell, and Anne, of whom the first is at John White, Esq. Upper-Wood House, Rawdon; the second is at Luddenden Foot; and the third is, I believe, at Scarborough, inditing perhaps a paper similar to this.

A scheme is at present in agitation for setting us up in a school of our own; as yet nothing is determined, but I hope and trust it may go on and prosper and answer our highest expectations. This day four years I wonder whether we shall still be dragging on in our present condition or established to our hearts' content. Time will show.

I guess that at the time appointed for the opening of this paper we, i.e., Charlotte, Anne, and I, shall be all merrily seated in our sitting room in some pleasant and flourishing seminary, having just gathered in for the midsummer holyday. Our debts will be paid off, and we shall have cash in hand to a considerable amount. Papa, Aunt, and Branwell will either have been or be coming to visit us. It will be a fine summer evening, very different from this bleak look-out, and Anne and I will perchance slip out into the garden for a few minutes to peruse our papers. I hope either this or something better will be the case.

The Gondolians are at present in a threatening state, but there is no open rupture as yet. All the princes and princesses of the Royalty are at the Palace of Instruction. I have a good many books on hand, but I am sorry to say that as usual I have made small progress with any. However, I have just made a new regularity paper! and I mean VERB SAP to do great things. And now I must close, sending from far an exhortation, "Courage, boys! Courage!" to exiled and harassed Anne, wishing she was here.

Anne's diary, although written in Thorp Green, echoes Emily's mood:

July the 30th, A.D. 1841.
This is Emily's birthday. She has now completed her 23rd year, and is, I believe, at home. Charlotte is a governess in the family of Mr. White. Branwell is a clerk in the railroad station at Luddenden Foot, and I am governess in the family of Mr. Robinson. I dislike the situation and wish to change it for another. I am now at Scarborough. My pupils are gone to bed and I am hastening to finish this before I follow them.

We are thinking of setting up a school of our own, but nothing definite is settled about it yet, and we do not know whether we shall be able to or not. I hope we shall, and I wonder what will be our conditions and how or where we shall be on this day four years hence; at which time, if all be well, I shall be 25 years and six months old, Emily will be 27 years old, Branwell 28 years and 1 month, and Charlotte 29 years and a quarter. We are now all separated and not likely to meet again for many a weary week, but are none of us ill that I know of, and we are all doing something for our own livelihood except Emily, who, however, is as busy as any of us, and in reality earns her food and raiment as much as we do.

> How little we know what we are
> How less what we may be!

Four years ago I was at school. Since then I have been a governess at Blake Hall, left it, come to Thorp Green, and seen the sea and York Minster. Emily has been a teacher at Miss Patchett's school and left it. Charlotte has left Miss Wooler's, been a governess at Mrs. Sidgwick's, left her, and gone to Mrs. White's. Branwell has given up painting, been a tutor in Cumberland, left it, and become a clerk on the railroad. Taby has left us. Martha Brown has come in her place. We have got Keeper, got a sweet little cat, and lost it, and also got a hawk. Got a wild goose which has flown away, and three tame ones, one of which has been killed. All these diversities, with many others, are things we did not expect or foresee in the July of 1837. What will the next four years bring forth? Providence only knows. But we ourselves have sustained very little alteration since that time. I have the same faults that I had then, only I have more vision and experience, and a little more self-possession than I then enjoyed. How will it be when we open this paper and the one Emily has written? I wonder whether the Gondolians will still be flourishing and what will be their condition. I am now engaged in writing the fourth volume of Solala Vernon's life.

For some time I have looked upon 25 as a sort of era in my existence. It may prove true presentiment, or it may be only a superstitious fancy; the latter seems more likely, but time will show.

Anne Bronte

Before Charlotte made further attempts to realize her vision of the school, she decided to delay. Various factors had decided Charlotte to arrange for Emily and herself to first study abroad. Mary Taylor's enthusiastic letters urged Charlotte to join her in Brussels.

When Mary Taylor, visiting her sister Martha in a school near Brussels, early in the summer of 1841, had extolled that city's cathedrals and works of art, Charlotte had been almost unbearably moved. As she wrote Ellen in early August:

> Mary's letter spoke of some of the pictures and cathedrals she had seen—pictures the most exquisite—cathedrals the most venerable. I hardly know what swelled to my throat as I read her letter; such a vehement impatience of restraint and steady work; such a strong wish for wings— wings such as wealth can furnish; such an urgent thirst to see, to know, to learn.

In Charlotte's mood of nostalgic yearning, her employers, paternally interested in Charlotte's plans, strongly urged Charlotte to first study abroad for at least six months. Charlotte, fired not only by the Taylors' experiences in Brussels, but by reading a batch of French novels lent by the Francophile Taylors, determined to join her friends in Brussels. In "extreme excitement," she wrote to Aunt Branwell and adroitly pointed out not only the undeniable practical benefits. But, sounding a more emotional note, she expressed the need to act with the daring which had brought Mr. Bronte from an obscure Irish village to Cambridge University, England. As she explained to her Aunt, through the British Embassy's chaplain in Brussels, a Mr. Jenkins, whose clergyman brother-in-law lived near Haworth, she could easily find an inexpensive Brussels school. Writing to Aunt Branwell on September 29th, she notes:

My friends recommend me, if I desire to secure permanent success, to delay the school for six months or longer, and to contrive to spend the intervening time in some school on the continent. They say schools in England are so numerous, competition so great that without some such superiority we shall probably have a very hard struggle and may fail in the end.

I would not go to France or Paris. I would go to Brussels in Belgium. Living there is little more than half as dear as in England, and the facilities for education are equal or superior to any other place in Europe. In half a year I could acquire a thorough familiarity with French. I could improve greatly in Italian and even get a dash of some other language . . . If I wrote to her (Mary Taylor), she with the assistance of Mrs. Jenkins, would be able to secure me a cheap, decent residence and respectable protection . . . She would make me acquainted with the city; and, with the assistance of her cousins, I should be introduced to connections far more improving, polished, and cultivated than any I have yet known.

These are advantages which would turn to real account, when we commenced a school; and, if Emily could share them with me, we could take a footing in the world which we could never do now. I say Emily instead of Anne; for Anne might take her turn, if our school answered . . . You always like to use your money to the best advantage; depend on it 50 or 100 pounds, thus laid out, would be well employed . . . I feel an absolute conviction it would be the making of us for life.

Papa will, perhaps, think it a wild and ambitious scheme; but who ever rose in the world without ambition? When he left Ireland (for) Cambridge University, he was as ambitious as I am now. I want US ALL to get on, and I know we have talents, and I want them to be turned to account.

As Charlotte explained to Ellen, she chose Emily rather than Anne, since the former, so long home-and-drudgery bound "deserved the reward." As she confided privately to Emily by letter, the original six months could be extended. If necessary, they could teach English.

Unfortunately, Emily's feelings about going to Brussels are unknown. But shortly after the Christmas holidays of 1841-42, and after some delay in finding a moderately priced Brussels school (cheaper Lille in France had been discussed as a possible alternative), Emily and Charlotte entered the Pensionnat Heger in Brussels. Its directors, Monsieur and Madame Heger, interested in the sisters' ambition to teach, had offered them inexpensive tuition.

Emily, one of a little Yorkshire party, which included Mr. Bronte (armed with a notebook in which he had listed useful French phrases and their pronunciation), Charlotte, Mary Taylor (en route to rejoin her sister), and her brother, Joe Taylor, left Haworth for London and Brussels on February 8th.

Anne remained, not too contentedly (i.e., according to her diary), in Thorp Green. Branwell was left, as he lamented to a friend, "to pursue the cold and malignant debauchery," either alone or with friends, "wild and wooly manufacturers" in Keighley and Bradford. It was his only escape from his lonely, dreary existence as a booking clerk in the one-room, wooden, shanty-like Luddenden Foot railroad station.

In London, Emily, despite her dislike of great cities (as Charlotte explained Emily's later refusal to accompany her to London, Emily "detested the artificial man of cities"), must have been enchanted by the rather shabby Holborn Inn where the Brontes spent a few nights. The Chapter Coffee House had been the meeting place for such great eighteenth century literary figures as the ill-fated poet, Thomas Chatterton, Dr. Samuel Johnson and Oliver Goldsmith. Certainly Emily was passionately interested in seeing the historical and artistic London landmarks. Mary Taylor later wrote to Mrs. Gaskell that both Emily and Charlotte were so determined "upon seeing all pictures and statues" and such sites as St. Paul's, that it had seemed that the party would be delayed in London indefinitely. And, as Miss Taylor commented about Emily, "Emily was like her (Charlotte) in these habits of mind," but independent from Charlotte in artistic taste and "never took her opinion but always had one to offer."

11
EMILY AND CHARLOTTE
IN BRUSSELS

Emily Brontë's nine months in Brussels had little effect on her as a human being or as a writer—except perhaps in a sheerly intellectual and scholastic sense. Indeed, Emily's life at the Pensionnat Heger (particularly viewed retrospectively), has an almost nightmarish quality of dislocation. Emily Bronte, dressed in her unbecoming, leg-of-mutton-sleeved, homemade clothes; monosyllabically reserved and direct; passionately endeared to home and homely living; with her independent religious beliefs and her Protestant mistrust of religious ritual in a large, fashionable Catholic school, was tragically misplaced.

The Pensionnat educated Brussels' *haute bourgeoisie*. Elaborately housed in a former seventeenth century mansion, built originally by the Infanta Isabella, it was in the Rue D'Isabelle which adjoined by a stone stairway Brussels' fashionable Rue Royale.

Here, in this foreign Catholic milieu, Emily was even more alienated than in Roe Head or Miss Patchett's schools. Indeed it was only by a tremendous battle of the will that she remained. As Charlotte described Emily here:

> The same suffering and conflict ensued, heightened by the strong recoil of her upright, heretic spirit from the Jesuitry of the foreign and Romish systems—once more

79

she rallied through the mere force of resolution with inward remorse and shame; she looked back on her former failures and resolved to conquer. But her effort was none the less painful . . . The victory cost her dear. She was never happy until she carried her hard won knowledge back to the remote English village; the old Parsonage house and the desolate Yorkshire hills.

But Emily's determination equalled her suffering. As Charlotte wrote to Ellen: "Emily worked like a horse and made rapid progress in French, German, music and drawing."

Quite realistically, Emily's and Charlotte's position as English, provincials, and Protestants in the Pensionnat was nearly untenable. The two Brontes, isolated, "in the midst of numbers," in Charlotte's words, remind one of enemy aliens living in a foreign land. And the natural barriers between them and the Pensionnat pupils were almost impassable. As Charlotte put it succinctly: "We have the brand of Anglicism and Protestantism upon us" and we "avoid and are avoided by the Belgian pupils."

Charlotte detested (or pretended to detest) the Belgian girls equally intensely. Emily, according to Charlotte, rarely spoke to them. Despising her fellow-pupils, en masse, Charlotte described them as temperamentally cold, basely mercenary, morally corrupt. Since the Belgians do not have "intellect, good nature nor good manners nor good feelings . . . they are nothing." Her attitude was reciprocated by the Belgians. Charlotte stated: "The Belgians hate the English."

Fortunately, Emily and Charlotte could escape to the relative privacy of their specially curtained off cubicles in the dormitory for which Aunt Branwell had generously paid extra. And in daytime recreation periods they retreated to the Pensionnat's large, continental-type, fruit-treed, rear garden. Its vine-covered arbour and *Allee Defendue*—a tree-lined path which bordered a wall separating the Pensionnat from the neighboring boy's academy, have been romantically described by Charlotte in *Villette*.

Emily and Charlotte found only the very few English pupils and an eccentric spinster teacher, a Mlle. Marie, in the least, "sympathique," in Charlotte's phrase. Particularly Laetitia Wheelwright, who became Charlotte's intimate friend. Miss Wheelwright, the daughter of a London doctor resident in Brussels, along with her four younger sisters (later Emily's piano pupils) was a day pupil. Charlotte had first noticed Miss Wheelwright approvingly when the latter rose in class and surveyed the Belgians disdainfully. As Charlotte wrote: "It was so very English." But this attitude if delightful to Charlotte could hardly endear her or Emily to the Belgians.

Probably Emily and Charlotte were drawn to Mlle. Marie for the same reason. This teacher was spiritually, if not by nationality, an alien here. As Charlotte described Mlle. Marie to Ellen:

> There are three teachers in the school. The first two have no particular character. Mlle. Marie is talented and original, but of repulsive and arbitrary manners, which have made the whole school—except Emily and myself, her bitter enemies.

Yet Emily's emotional isolation here was not entirely unbroken. A slightly older Belgian pupil, a Mlle. de Bassompierre, in a memoir, remembered Emily as less "brillante" but more "sympathique" than Charlotte. The comment is brief. But Emily must have shown this girl her warm, human aspect, which she usually revealed only in her love of nature and of animals. Long after Emily's death, this lady still had a memento which Emily had given her, a signed drawing of a Yorkshire-like landscape—a lone, bare-branched pine tree against a sombre sky, which Emily had sketched in the Pensionnat garden.

Otherwise, Brussels must have been unrelievedly dreary

for Emily who lived in Charlotte's shadow. It had none of the interest it had for Charlotte. Emily barely understood French. As Charlotte explained:

> Emily has great difficulties to contend with—far greater than I have had. Indeed to come to a French school one ought previously to have acquired a considerable knowledge of the French language—otherwise they will lose a great deal of time.

Brussels was not a happy release from detested governessing for Emily but an exile from her native moorland to which she was deeply endeared. Emily entirely lacked Charlotte's romantic passion for foreign travel, hence Brussels was a less magical experience. The Brontes' various English friends, the Jenkinses, the Wheelwrights, and the Dixons (the Taylors' cousins), all spoke of Emily as silent and despondent. Mary Taylor, describing to Ellen a Sunday evening which she spent with Emily and Charlotte, after a six-mile walk to the Protestant cemetery to visit her late sister Martha's grave (who had died suddenly and tragically), stated that Emily did not utter a word.

Above all, Brussels did not provide Emily with creative nourishment. In the Pensionnat background and in Constantin Heger (the school's co-director and rhetoric teacher), Charlotte found fascinating material which she used in two novels. Mr. Heger was the first distinguished teacher to encourage Charlotte. She immediately idealized him as her literary "Maitre," if not her romantic love, as many biographers claim. Mr. Heger, in Charlotte's various descriptions, was temperamental, vitriolic, physically ugly but passionately dedicated to teaching.

Charlotte's adulation was probably an affair of the mind and the imagination rather than of the heart. Un-romantic in appearance, Charlotte once described him, probably aptly, during one of his classroom rages, as "an insane Tomcat."

Unfortunately, Mr. Heger did not inspire Emily. Charlotte wrote that Mr. Heger and Emily "did not draw well together at all." Emily did not have Charlotte's reverence for learning. Charlotte once stated that Emily wrote solely from "intuition" and direct "observation" and Emily had no interest in "filling her pitcher at the well-springs of other minds." Monsieur, like many gifted scholars, was academic, concerned with teaching traditional literary values. From one of his notes on the margin of a theme by Charlotte, in which she had described genius as "a gift of God," he obviously believed that literary talent was a plant, in itself valueless, except as trimmed into shape by traditional forms. Mr. Heger had written: "Genius without study; without art; without knowledge of what has been done is force without a lever—a musician with only an untuned piano."

But despite Mr. Heger's disapproval (he later wrote to Mrs. Gaskell that Emily selfishly dominated Charlotte), he did dimly perceive, rather as one does a distant, unfamiliar object, the shadowy outlines of Emily's literary greatness. To Mrs. Gaskell, he pointed out aspects of Emily's genius which she did not fulfill, even in *Wuthering Heights*. Mr. Heger wrote:

> She should have been a man—a great navigator. Her powerful reason would have deduced new spheres of discovery from the knowledge of the old; and her strong imperious will would never have been daunted by opposition or difficulty; never would have given way but with life. And yet moreover, her faculty of imagination was such that if she had written a history, her view of scenes and characters would have been so vivid, and so powerfully expressed and supported by such a show of argument, that it would have dominated the reader whatever might have been his previous opinions or his cooler perceptions of its truth.

From Mr. Heger's teaching, Emily's only gain for her writing was indirect. Mr. Heger taught writing by having his students imitate the styles of such writers as Bossuet, Victor Hugo, etc.

Emily, already conscious of her direction as a writer, refused. She claimed that it would destroy her own originality. Indeed, Emily's very distinction of mind was probably a cause of her boredom in Brussels.

To Emily, as a novelist, both Mr. Heger's pedagogy and the life at the Pensionnat were profoundly irrelevant. Neither could give her inspiration or material. Emily was a poetic visionary rather than a romantic naturalist like Charlotte, who based two novels, *The Professor* and *Villette*, on her Pensionnat experiences. But in Emily's novel or her poems there is no trace of her personal life in Brussels. (Typically, Charlotte wrote about thirty poems here, while Emily wrote only three mediocre poems, one of which was finished in Haworth.)

Much like her twentieth century literary descendant, D. H. Lawrence, Emily was a philosophic, poetic novelist, preoccupied with man's inner emotions. Like D. H. Lawrence, she was concerned with writing a moral epic on the eternal themes of man's primal emotions: great loves, hates, redemption, and revenge. Certainly the artificial atmosphere of the Pensionnat was not a usable background. The Belgian young ladies were hardly potential fictional characters for the author of *Wuthering Heights*. Charlotte claimed that the Belgian-Flemish temperament was abnormally passionless and phlegmatic. As Charlotte complained in a letter: "Nobody gets into a passion here. The phlegm that thickens their blood is too gluey to boil."

Emily needed a less limited, more natural background. An English moorland town, with its undenatured, passion-ridden individualists, set against a background of the eternal laws of nature; the turning seasons with the miracle of renewal; storm and sunlight; the hidden, chemical mechanism which miraculously adjusts the rate of growth, color, and form of grass, trees and flowers, was (as in much of Lawrence's writing), an indispensable background.

Yet Emily in her own instinctive way found direction in reading German novels here. Many biographers have even claimed that *Wuthering Heights* was modelled on a New German Romanticist novel: E. T. Hoffman's *The Entail.* The German novel's mood of metaphysical brooding and ghostly melodrama probably planted in Emily the idea to adapt her massive genius (hitherto expressed only in poetry) to the novel. One remembers the almost supernatural character of Heathcliff's evil-doing. And such super-real, ghostly episodes as when Heathcliff returning to Wuthering Heights from Cathy Linton's grave, in his emotional delirium, really believes that he will find Cathy at The Heights, not merely in the spirit but in the flesh.

Charlotte's and Emily's months in Brussels were ended by Aunt Branwell's death, which abruptly recalled the two Brontes to Haworth. During the Brontes' second six months, Monsieur Heger had offered them part-time jobs as teachers (Charlotte taught French—Emily piano) in return for free board and tuition. Emily had become a competent piano teacher. As Monsieur lamented to Patrick Bronte about interruption to the Brontes' promising teaching careers: "De ja elle (Emily) avait des petites eleves" and "Elle (Emily) perdait un reste d'ignorance et de timidite."

Had Emily remained the intended second six months, would she have become an English music teacher in a Belgian school rather than the author of *Wuthering Heights?* Probably not. In Emily Bronte's life, Aunt's death was a timely, chance event, which though it appears to alter the direction of a life, is merely the outward factor which releases things which have long been embryonic.

Indeed, the quick departure from the Pensionnat, was to Emily probably a miraculous escape from a dreaded future.

When on November 2nd they had word that Aunt was seriously ill, they consulted Monsieur and Madame Heger and decided to leave immediately for Haworth. The next day they had news of her death, which might conceivably have delayed their plans. Yet, three days later they packed their newly bought, iron-banded, Belgian trunks and departed for Antwerp, London and Haworth. On the morning of the 8th they had reached the parsonage.

When early next year Charlotte returned, alone, to Brussels, to teach, Emily had no desire to join her. True, Mr. Bronte was then seriously disabled by failing eyesight, which necessitated Emily's or Charlotte's (Anne was in Thorp Green) being in Haworth. But, although Charlotte's subsequent letters from Brussels were filled with detailed self-reproaches at leaving Mr. Bronte, there is no hint that either Emily or Charlotte regretted that Emily had remained in Haworth.

12

EMILY IN HAWORTH
CHARLOTTE IN BRUSSELS
EMILY MATURES

DESPITE Aunt Branwell's death, Emily's and Charlotte's lives on their return from Brussels remained much unchanged. Her funeral had occurred while they were still en route to Haworth. Charlotte, writing to Ellen, to urge the latter to visit them, shortly after their return in November, 1842, stated: "Do not fear to find us melancholy or depressed. We are much the same."

Actually, the only important effect of Miss Branwell's death—particularly to Emily and Charlotte, who were not particularly emotionally close to her—was purely financial. For the tiny capital (between three and four hundred pounds, with an annual income of forty pounds) which each sister, along with a Cornish cousin, inherited, paid for publishing their first books. Branwell, Aunt's "favorite," had been disinherited with a "Japanese dressing box," probably because of his alcoholism. But Emily's inheritance was the means for her first appearance in print—the publication of her poems in a joint book of verse by the three sisters, for which they paid the costs—which in turn led to the writing of *Wuthering Heights*, for which she also paid part of the publication costs (shared by Anne) when it appeared in the same volume with Anne's *Agnes Grey*.

Psychologically, to Emily the tiny income must have given

a new, inner freedom. Both in allaying her restless, guilt feelings, caused by her self-styled "idleness" in Haworth and in lessening the threat of her creative energies being possibly channeled into teaching or governessing.

Yet, if Aunt's death did not have an emotionally depressing effect in the next phase in Emily's life, during which her finest poems and *Wuthering Heights* were written, the mental climate in Haworth was, for other reasons, particularly desolate.

Mr. Bronte's curate, the companionable William Weightman, had died about two months before Emily's and Charlotte's return from Brussels, from (like Aunt) what was then termed an internal obstruction, probably in modern medicine, appendicitis. Mr. Bronte was now nearly blind.

Branwell's debaucheries and his neglect of duty in the Luddenden Foot Railway Station had resulted in muddled accounts and in thievery by a railroad porter. Although Branwell had not been directly implicated, he had resigned in dishonor. In the subsequent months, alone at the parsonage, he had partially recovered a more normal morale. As he wrote a friend in the late Spring of 1842:

> . . . my recovery from ALMOST insanity. After experiencing, since my return home, extreme pain and illness with mental depression—I have at length acquired health and strength and soundness of mind. I can now speak cheerfully and enjoy the company of another without the stimulus of six glasses of whiskey.

But, alcohol- and opium-ridden, he lingered, futureless, at the parsonage. His recent deathbed vigils at the bedside of two loved beings, Aunt and Mr. Weightman, had intensified his self-pity and despair. Now, the reverse of his former unnatural, almost paranoic, hopefulness, belatedly realistic, his inordinate self-belief had become dangerously deflated. He continued to write poems and narratives. But in replying to his friend, F. Grundy, about the literary encouragement of a noted poet, James Montgomery, who had admired his writing, he writes: "They give me plenty of puff and praise. All very well, but I have little conceit of myself."

Yet, ironically, Branwell had recently had his two main literary successes. His poem, "The Afghan War" (oddly, the first Bronte writing to appear in print), had been published in *The Leeds Intelligencer* (May, 1842), under a pseudonym, Northangerland. And Samuel Coleridge's son, Hartley, whom Branwell had met in Ambleside, in June, 1840, while Branwell had been a tutor in Cumberland, the Lake District, had admired Branwell's translation of two odes of Horace. The English poet, John Drinkwater, rated Branwell's translation along with a few of Branwell's lyrics as not only Branwell's finest work but among the finest in English. Yet Branwell's present outlook was non-existent. A passing impulse to enter the ministry, doubtless in imitation of Mr. Bronte, had been, on serious reflection, rejected. As Branwell wrote to a friend, in the humility of his growing self-knowledge, "I have not one mental qualification save, perhaps, hypocrisy."

He still retained flashes of his earlier, so tragically misdirected fire and talent, which was now obviously in embers. While Branwell was still in Luddenden Foot, F. Grundy, after a visit with him, drew an admirably revealing portrait of this self-destroyed artist with his disintegrating talent. Grundy, vividly portrayed Branwell's physical appearance:

> Insignificantly small, one of his life's trials . . . his mass of red hair brushed high off his forehead to help his height —his great, bumpy, intellectual forehead, nearly half the size of his whole facial contour—small, ferrety eyes, deep sunk and still further hidden by never-removed spectacles!

And, as he listened to Branwell's brilliant talk, noted, "What a splendid specimen of brain power running wild—what glorious talent he still had to waste."

When Emily returned to the parsonage from Brussels, Branwell, with his now more limited ambitions, desired merely activity—an escape from his present, death-in-life stagnation in Haworth. As he had complained to Grundy, in pleading for aid in obtaining another railway post, he felt that the recovery of his mental equilibrium was:

> retarded by having nothing to listen to except the wind moaning among old chimneys and older ash trees; nothing to look at except heathery hills; no one to speak to except crabbed old Greeks and Romans who have been dust the last 5,000 years.

In Branwell's 1842 deadlock, a post which Anne obtained for him as tutor to the only son of her present employer, Rev. Robinson, seemed ironically enough, in the light of future events, a possible solution. Branwell, according to his friend, Leyland, with renewed hope returned with Anne to Thorp Green, at the end of the (1842-43) Christmas holidays.

Charlotte's life was at an almost equally tragic and muddled mental impasse. In returning to Brussels, Charlotte made one of the few decisions which she admittedly bitterly regretted. As she later wrote to Ellen: "I returned to Brussels after Aunt's death against my conscience, prompted by an irresistible impulse." Disregarding an inner voice, she listened, instead, to that of Monsieur Heger. For the latter had written to Mr. Bronte that further study and experience were essential to Charlotte's teaching career. She accepted the Heger's rather meagre offer of sixteen pounds yearly salary to teach English, paying extra for German lessons.

After a half-hearted attempt to persuade Ellen to join her, Charlotte, again, left for Brussels on January 27th, 1843. Not reaching London until evening, rather than spend an unchaperoned night, with rare initiative she had herself rowed alongside the Ostend channel boat and had insisted on being put aboard. After this dramatic midnight Thames embarkation (which she recreated in her novel, *Villette*) Charlotte was again in Brussels.

But her delight in returning to Brussels was destined to be brief. As she later admitted to Ellen, she "was punished for my selfish folly by a withdrawal for more than two years of happiness and peace of mind."

In Emily's and in Mary Taylor's absences (the latter was now studying in Germany), burdened by long hours of teaching, by her equivocal relationship to the Hegers (emotionally dependent on Monsieur as a literary "maitre" and her "one true friend," which Madame Heger interpreted, perhaps rightly, as romantic love, her former intimacy had dwindled), and by her fears about her uncertain future, Charlotte sank again as she had at Dewsbury Moor School into a state of morbid melancholia. Her celebrated Catholic Confession letter to Emily was pathetic evidence of her present psychic and emotional impasse in Brussels. As she described the episode to Emily, when she was wandering alone during the summer holiday in the warm, empty Brussels' streets, in order to escape the dreary Pensionnat with its large, deserted classrooms, in her disorientation this ingrained Protestant had drifted into St. Gudule, a Catholic church. And out of sheer loneliness, boredom, and perhaps inward guilt at not doing her duty at the parsonage, she had confessed to a Catholic priest.

Charlotte, in one of her various letters which alarmed Emily, movingly described the incident, on September 2nd, 1843:

> Yesterday I went on a pilgrimage to the cemetery. When I came back it was evening, but I had such a repugnance to return to the house which contained nothing I cared for, I

still kept threading the streets in the neighborhood of the
Rue D'Isabelle. I found myself opposite St. Gudule and the
bell whose voice you know began to toll for evening Salut.
I went in quite alone—wandered about the aisles, still I
could not leave the church, or force myself to go home,
the school, I mean. An odd whim came into my head. In
two Confessionals, I saw a priest. I felt as if I did not care
what I did, provided it was absolutely not wrong and that it
served to vary my life and yield a moment's interest. I took
a fancy to change myself into a Catholic and go and make a
real Confession to see what it was like—knowing me as you
do, you will think this odd, but when people are by themselves, they have singular fancies. I did not know a word of
the formula with which they always begin their Confession,
I felt precisely as I did when alone on the Thames at midnight. I actually did confess—a real confession. Of course,
the adventure stopped there. I hope I will never see the
Priest again. I think you had better not tell Papa. He will
not understand that it is only a freak and will perhaps think
that I am going to be a Catholic.

But, fortunately, in the end, Emily's fears that Charlotte
might, eventually, sink into a lethargy below the level of action, were not realized. Emily, in one of her very rare letters,
had even been moved to write Ellen to urge her to go to Brussels and bring Charlotte home. Emily, in May, 1843, reasoned:
"Otherwise, she might vegetate there till the age of Methu-
selah for mere lack of courage to face the voyage."

Mary Taylor, who knew about Charlotte's state of mind,
by letter, was even more apprehensive. As she later described
it to Mrs. Gaskell:

Her life became monotonous and she fell into the same
hopeless state as at Miss Wooler's. I wrote, urging her to
go home or elsewhere, that if she sank into deeper gloom
she would soon not have the energy to go.

But Charlotte delayed, as she semi-ironically wrote Ellen, because she dreaded "becoming an aged person on the parish."

In her nostalgia for home, in December, 1843, she finally wrote Emily that she intended to return to Haworth. And a few days after New Year's Day, Charlotte, bearing a diploma especially sealed by Monsieur with the Athenee Royale seal, a Brussels' lace collar and blouse and an inward sadness at leaving Monsieur, had reached Haworth. ("It grieved me to leave so true a friend," as she wrote to Ellen.)

In Haworth, the Brontes' outlook loomed hopelessly dismal. Mr. Bronte, nearly blind, was now, as Charlotte wrote to Monsieur, unable to read or write. He had become a semi-invalid. Branwell, during his holidays from Thorp Green, at the parsonage alternated between violently extremist moods of guilt and depression and of equally unbalanced hope.

Emily's and Charlotte's former unique "polar star of hope," the Bronte school, for which Charlotte's heroic efforts had at last qualified them, ironically must now be postponed indefinitely. As Charlotte dejectedly explained to Ellen, shortly after her return to Haworth in January, 1844:

> Everyone expects that I would start a school. In truth, it is what I would wish to do. I desire it above all things. I have sufficient cash. And, I hope now sufficient qualifications. Yet, I cannot permit myself to touch the object which seems within my reach and which I have been so long straining to attain. It is on Papa's account. He is losing his sight. I ought not to be away from him.

For the same reason, a hundred-pounds-a-year senior teachership in a Manchester school was refused by Charlotte a few months later. Yet, in the very closing of avenues of exit from the parsonage to Charlotte, and to Emily the writing of their novels in Haworth was being made a reality.

But, in her present despondency, Charlotte was psychically at her lowest ebb. As this former spearhead of ambition for all the Brontes writes to Ellen, early in 1844: "Something which used to be enthusiasm is tamed and broken. I have fewer illusions! Haworth is a lonely, quiet spot buried away from the world." And writing to Ellen, in February, 1845, of a farewell visit to her friends, the Taylors, before Mary Taylor departed for New Zealand, she admitted:

> I spent a week at Hunsworth, not very pleasantly; head-ache, sickliness and flatness of spirits made me a poor companion, a sad drag. I never was so fortunate to rally even for a single hour. I perceive that I have too little life in me, nowadays, to be fit company for any except very quiet people.

Charlotte's nearly defeated state of mind had been intensified by her long-drawn-out, painful relationship to Monsieur Heger, to whose idealized memory she persisted in clinging as to an utterly unrealistic, self-willed image. It had resulted in the forcible end (after repeated warnings from Monsieur) of their correspondence.

Perhaps even more serious was the temporary renunciation of her career as a novelist, due, as she wrote Monsieur, to her weakening eyesight. In despair, Charlotte again reluctantly turned to teaching. In July, 1844, she sadly explained to her "Maitre":

> Formerly I passed whole days and weeks and months in writing, not wholly without result, for Southey and Coleridge—two of our best authors, to whom I sent certain manuscripts, were good enough to express their approval; but now my sight is too weak to write, were I to write much I should become blind. This weakness of sight is a terrible hindrance to me. Otherwise, I should write a book, and I should dedicate it to my Literature Master. But this cannot be. The career of letters is closed to me—only that

of teaching is open. It does not offer the same attractions. Nevertheless, I shall enter it and if I do not go far it shall not be for want of industry.

Fortunately Charlotte's brave, final effort to renew the Bronte school proved abortive. Believing, indeed it was a main tenet of her philosophy, that the perpetual battle with reality and with oneself is in itself salutary (in her own words: "Effort must be beneficial whatever the result" and "a task without difficulty is also without merit—the great interest in triumphing over obstacles"), she attempted to revive the Bronte school idea.

In May, 1844, the Bronte sisters again discussed the school. But Charlotte compromised on Haworth. She planned to transform the parsonage, by adding a wing, into a miniature boarding school, housing five or six pupils. In one of her letters to Monsieur, in July, 1844, in which she described the future parsonage school, she revealed the essential difference in mentality and in temperament between Emily and herself, and the very minor part which Emily would play in Charlotte's proposed school. Charlotte writes:

> Our parsonage is rather a large house, with a few alterations there will be room for five or six boarders. If I could find this number of children of good family, I should devote myself to their education. Emily does not care much for teaching, but she would look after the housekeeping, and, although something of a recluse, she is too good-hearted not to do all she could for the well-being of the children. Moreover, she is very generous, and as for economy, strictness and diligent order, all of them essential in a school, I willingly take that upon myself. That, Monsieur, is my plan, which I have already explained to my father and which he approves. It only remains to find pupils, rather a difficult thing, for we live rather far from towns, and

people do not greatly care about crossing the hills which form a barrier around us.

The barrier did, in fact, prove impassable. Although Charlotte, Emily and Anne printed and distributed advertising circulars, with the aid of half a dozen friends, including the faithful Ellen, and personally interviewed parents, they did not enlist even a single pupil. Charlotte's former employer, Mr. White, would have entered his daughters. But they had been already "promised." But, as a lady in Keighley, whose daughters had been also already entered in a school, pointed out to Charlotte (as Charlotte told Mrs. Gaskell), Haworth, ringed by hills, was fatally remote and inaccessible. It was a handicap which this lady believed could not be offset, even by the Brontes' very moderate fees—about half the usual charge. By Autumn (October, 1844) the scheme was definitely renounced. Yet, Charlotte at least, with typical fortitude, was not unduly depressed. She was "glad that we made the attempt and will not be cast down because it has not been successful. It teaches us experience of and knowledge of the world."

Since Emily's interest was obviously merely a reflection of Charlotte's, and primarily financial, she was quite frankly relieved. In her July 30th, 1845, Birthday Note, Emily writes:

> It (the school) was found no go. Now I don't desire a school at all, and none of us have any great longing for it. We have cash enough for present wants with a prospect of accumulation.

For Emily was far more singly preoccupied with her own writing than Charlotte. In February, 1844, Emily had copied her poems, written like Emily Dickinson's on scattered, loose pieces of paper, into two notebooks. One included her Gondal poems; the second untitled notebook, her non-Gondal, personal poems. Less mature than Charlotte, she was still absorbed in her Gondal tales. For in Emily's above-noted diary, written a few days after one of her rare excursions away from Haworth (a three-day walking tour with Anne, during which they inspected York Cathedral and impersonated various Gondal characters as they tramped through the English countryside), she writes that she was then composing a Gondal book: *A History of the First War*.

Furthermore, despite the increasing shadows in Charlotte's and in Branwell's lives, and negatively in her own life, Emily was, as she also noted, "undesponding." For, for whatever obscure reasons, perhaps merely with time passing, or because she now accepted the Brontes' defeats in the real world, or because she was maturing and fulfilling herself as a poet, Emily's mystique had flowered into a spiritual pantheism—a mystic union and reverent belief in a Universal Spirit, a timeless enduring essence; a "presence" beyond religious creed; human ills; ordinary concepts of good and evil; even personal Death. In her poems she described it variously as a "Spirit," "Deity," "Eternity," "the Unseen," "Earth." Her deeper spiritual poise is reflected in the greater inner power, emotional complexity of these later poems. Among her finest lyrics, "Death," "No Coward Soul," "The Prisoner," "The Philosopher," and her untitled "Last Lines," were written during this period.

In one of her most celebrated poems, "No Coward Soul," (January 2nd, 1846), the Spirit is a "God Within," a "Deity," who transcends religious creed and death.

> No coward soul is mine
> No trembler in the world's storm-troubled sphere
> I see Heaven's glories shine
> And Faith shines equal arming me from Fear.
>
> O God within my breast
> Almighty ever-present Deity
> Life that in me has rest
> As I undying Life, have power in Thee

Vain are the thousand creeds
That move men's hearts, unutterably vain,
Worthless as withered weeds
Or idlest froth amid the boundless main

To waken doubt in one
Holding so fast by thy infinity
So surely anchored on
The steadfast rock of Immortality

With wide-embracing love
Thy spirit animates eternal years
Pervades and broods above,
Changes, sustains, dissolves, creates and rears

Though Earth and moon were gone
And suns and universes ceased to be
And thou wert left alone
Every existence would exist in thee

There is not room for Death
Nor atom that his might could render void
Since thou art Being and Breath
And what thou art may never be destroyed.

And, in two poems, the "Spirit" compensates for personal disillusion. In a poem on Death (April 10th, 1845) the Spirit is "Eternity":

Death, that struck when I was most confiding
In my certain Faith of Joy to be,
Strike again, Time's withered branch dividing
From the fresh root of Eternity!

Leaves, upon Time's branch, were growing brightly,
Full of sap and full of silver dew;
Birds, beneath its shelter, gathered nightly;
Daily, round its flowers, the wild bees flew.

Sorrow passed and plucked the golden blossom,
Guilt stripped off the foliage in its pride;
But, within its parent's kindly bosom,
Flowed forever Life's restoring tide.

Little mourned I for the parted Gladness,
For the vacant nest and silent song;
Hope was there and laughed me out of sadness,
Whispering, "Winter will not linger long."

And behold, with tenfold increase blessing
Spring adorned the beauty-burdened spray;
Wind and rain and fervent heat caressing
Lavished glory on its second May.

High it rose; no winged grief could sweep it;
Sin was scared to distance with its shine;
Love and its own life had power to keep it
From all wrong, from every blight but thine!

Heartless death, the young leaves droop and languish!
Evening's gentle air may still restore—
No: the morning sunshine mocks my anguish—
Time for me must never blossom more!

Strike it down, that other boughs may flourish
Where that perished sapling used to be;
Thus, at least, its mouldering corpse will nourish
That from which it sprung—Eternity.

In "The Philosopher," Emily renounces even thought. She laments not having discovered earlier a healing "seer," "a spirit standing," who miraculously reconciles "divided sources." Were these "divided sources," perhaps, the conflicts and divisions among the Brontes? Written on February 3rd, 1845, it reads in part:

Enough of Thought, Philosopher;
Too long hast thou been dreaming

O for the time when I shall sleep
Without identity,
And never care how rain may steep
Or snow may cover me!

No promised Heaven, these wild desires
Could all or half fulfill;
No threatened Hell, with quenchless fires,
Subdue this quenchless will!

—so said I, and still say the same;
—Still to my Death will say—
Three Gods within this little frame
Are warring night and day.

Heaven could not hold them all, and yet
They all are held in me
And must be mine till I forget
My present entity.

O for the time when in my breast
Their struggles will be o'er;
O for the day when I shall rest,
And never suffer more!

I saw a Spirit standing, Man
Where thou dost stand—an hour ago;
And round his feet, three rivers ran
Of equal depth and equal flow—

A Golden stream, and one like blood,
And one like Sapphire, seemed to be,
But where they joined their triple flood
It tumbled in an inky sea.

The Spirit bent his dazzling gaze
Down on that Ocean's gloomy night,
Then—kindling all with sudden blaze,
The glad deep sparkled wide and bright—
White as the sun; far, far more fair
Than the divided sources were!

—And even for that Spirit, Seer,
I've watched and sought my lifetime long;
Sought him in Heaven, Hell, Earth and Air,
An endless search—and always wrong!

Had I but seen his glorious eye
ONCE light the clouds that wilder me,
I ne'er had raised this coward cry
To cease to think and cease to be—

I ne'er had called oblivion blest,
Nor stretching eager hands to Death
Implored to change for lifeless rest
This sentient soul, this living breath.

In her undated poem (which Charlotte titled "Last Lines,"
and which she claimed was Emily's last poem), she epitomizes
her final mystique. The "Spirit," still a reconciler, in the last
stanza is identified with "Earth"—Nature.

What have those lonely mountains worth revealing?
More glory and more grief than I can tell:
The earth that wakes ONE human heart to feeling
Can centre both the worlds of Heaven and Hell.

In Emily's Birthday Diary, July 30th, 1845, she also strikes
a new note of inner harmony. She is now:

quite contented . . . having learned to make the most of
the present and long for the future with less fidgetiness that
I cannot do all I wish . . . merely desiring that everybody could be as comfortable as myself and as undesponding, and then we should have a very tolerable world of it.

And of Branwell, hitherto a source of unhappy inner conflict, though he had just been dismissed by his employer, Mr.
Robinson, for alleged scandalous relations with the latter's
wife, Emily merely writes, ". . . who, I hope, will be better
and do better hereafter."

Emily's diary reads:

HAWORTH, THURSDAY, JULY 30, 1845.

My birthday—showery, breezy, cool. I am twenty-seven years old today. This morning Anne and I opened the papers we wrote four years since, on my twenty-third birthday. This paper we intend, if all be well, to open on my thirtieth—three years hence, in 1848. Since the 1841 paper the following events have taken place. Our school scheme has been abandoned, and instead Charlotte and I went to Brussels on the 8th of February, 1842. Branwell left his place at Luddenden Foot. C. and I returned from Brussels, November 8th, 1842, in consequence of Aunt's death. Branwell went to Thorp Green as a tutor, where Anne still continued, January, 1843. Charlotte returned to Brussels the same month, and after staying a year, came back again on New Year's Day, 1844. Anne left her situation at Thorp Green of her own accord, June 1845. Anne and I went on our first long journey by ourselves together, leaving home on the 30th of June, Monday, sleeping at York, returning to Keighley Tuesday evening, sleeping there and walking home on Wednesday morning. Though the weather was broken we enjoyed ourselves very much, except during the few hours at Bradford. And during our excursion we were, Ronald Macalgin, Henry Angora, Juliet Augusteena, Rosabella Esmaldan, Ella and Julian Egremont, Catharine Navarre, and Cordelia Fitzaphnold, escaping from the palaces of instruction to join the Royalists who are hard driven at present by the victorious Republicans. The Gondals still flourish bright as ever. I am at present writing a work on the first wars. Anne has been writing some articles on this, and a book by Henry Sophona. We intend sticking firm by the rascals as long as they delight us, which I am glad to say they do at present. I should have mentioned that last summer the school scheme was revived in full vigor. We had prospectuses printed, dispatched letters to all acquaintances imparting our plans, and did our little all but it was found no go. Now I don't desire a school at all, and none of us have any great longing for it. We have cash enough for our present wants, with a prospect of accumulation. We are all in decent health, only that Papa has a complaint in his eyes, and with the exception of B., who, I hope will be better and do better hereafter. I am quite contented with myself: not as idle as formerly, altogether as hearty, and having learned to make the most of the present and long for the future with less fidgetiness that I cannot do all I wish; seldom or never troubled with nothing to do, and merely desiring that everybody could be as comfortable as myself and as undesponding, and then we should have a very tolerable world of it. By mistake I find we have opened the paper on the 31st instead of the 30th. Yesterday was such a day as this, but the morning was divine. Tabby who was gone in our last paper, is come back, and has lived with us two years and a half, and is in good health. Martha, who also departed, is here too. We have got Flossy; got and lost Tiger; lost the hawk Hero, which, with the geese, was given away, and is doubtless dead, for when I came back from Brussels, I enquired on all hands and could hear nothing of him. Tiger died early last year. Keeper and Flossy are well, also the canary acquired four years since. We are now all at home, and likely to be there some time. Branwell went to Liverpool on Tuesday to stay a week. Tabby has just been teasing me to turn as formerly to "pillopitate." Anne and I should have picked the black currants if it had been fine and sunshiny. I must hurry off now to my turning and ironing. I have plenty of work on hand, and writing, and am altogether full of business. With best wishes for the whole house till 1848, July 30th, and as much longer as may be,—I conclude.

Anne's diary also presents a tranquil picture of Emily.

THURSDAY, JULY THE 31ST, 1845:

Yesterday was Emily's birthday, and the time when we should have opened our 1841 paper, but by mistake we opened it today instead. How many things have happened since it was written—some pleasant, some far otherwise. Yet I was then at Thorp Green, and now I am only just escaped from it. I was wishing to leave it then, and if I had known that I had four years longer to stay, how wretched I should have been; but during my stay I have had some very unpleasant and undreamt-of experience of human nature. Others have seen more changes. Charlotte has been at Mr. White's and been twice to Brussels, where she stayed each time nearly a year. Branwell has left Ludden-den Foot, and been a tutor at Thorp Green, and had much tribulation and ill health. He was very ill on Thursday but he went with John Brown to Liverpool, where he now is, I suppose; and we hope he will be better and do better in the future. This is a dismal, cloudy, wet evening. We have had so far a very cold, wet summer. Charlotte has lately been to Hathersage, in Derbyshire, on a visit of three weeks to Ellen Nussey. She is now sitting sewing in the dining room. Emily is ironing upstairs. I am sitting in the dining room in the rocking-chair before the fire with my feet on the fender. Papa is in the parlour. Tabby and Martha are, I think, in the kitchen. Keeper and Flossy are, I do not know where. Little Dick is hopping in his cage. When the last paper was written we were thinking of setting up a school. The scheme has been dropt, and long after taken up again, and dropt again, because we could not get pupils. Charlotte is thinking about getting another situation. She wishes to go to Paris. Will she go? She has let Flossy in, by-the-by, and he is now lying on the sofa. Emily is engaged in writing the Emperor Julius' Life. She has read some of it, and I want very much to hear the rest. She is writing some poetry too. I wonder what it is about? I have begun the third volume of PASSAGES IN THE LIFE OF AN INDIVIDUAL. I wish I had finished it. This afternoon I began to set about making my grey figured silk frock that was dyed at Keighley. What sort of a hand shall I make of it? I want to get a habit of early rising. Shall I succeed? We have not yet finished our GONDAL CHRONICLES that we began three years and a half ago. When will they be done? The Gondals are at present in a sad state. The Republicans are uppermost, but the Royalists are not quite overcome. The young sovereign with their brothers and sisters, are still at the Palace of Instruction. The Unique Society, about half a year ago, were wrecked on a desert island as they were returning from Gaul. They are still there but we have not played at them much yet. The Gondals in general are not in first-rate playing condition. Will they improve? I wonder how we shall all be, and where and how situated, on the thirtieth of July 1848, when, if we are all alive, Emily will be just 30, I shall be in my 29th year, Charlotte in her 33rd, and Branwell in his 32nd; and what changes shall we have seen and known; and shall we be much changed ourselves? I hope not, for the worse at least. I for my part, cannot well be flatter or older in mind than I am now. Hoping for the best, I conclude.

But the calm atmosphere of Emily's life at the parsonage was shortly to be violently dispelled. Branwell's dismissal was the signal for his last tragic phase—his disastrous love for Mrs. Robinson. The affair turned Branwell into a raving, drunken maniac and infested the parsonage wih melodrama until Branwell died. Yet it did not disrupt Emily's inner poise. Within a very few months after its first, violent outbreak she began to write *Wuthering Heights*—which, indeed, it fuelled.

13

BRANWELL
MRS. ROBINSON
WUTHERING HEIGHTS

Rumors of the approaching Branwell-Mrs. Robinson debacle had reached the parsonage months before its first, actual, dramatic eruption and its even more terrible repercussions. During the previous winter of 1844-45, Anne's letters had hinted at the reasons behind Branwell's recent odd behavior in Haworth and in Thorp Green. When Anne returned permanently to the parsonage in the spring, she had related her pupils' sordid blackmailing of their mother about her supposed relations with their brother's tutor. She admitted that in reality, in Anne's words, "There was something between them." In Charlotte's memorable words, "the season of distress and disquietude" which overhung the parsonage until Branwell's death, important because it was the psychological atmosphere in which *Wuthering Heights* was to be written and patently provided Emily with its dramatic nucleus, began almost immediately after Branwell had returned alone to Thorp Green. Strangely enough, Charlotte, while en route to Haworth from a holiday in Derbyshire with Ellen, had had an odd premonition. While pleasantly engaged in chatting in French with a Frenchman on the train, she had experienced a feeling of impending disaster (as she recalled in a letter).

Indeed, during Charlotte's holiday, Branwell, supposedly

in the midst of his tutoring duties in Thorp Green, had unexpectedly turned up at the parsonage on July 17th, even
more emotionally distraught and dishevelled than usual. His
arrival had been quickly followed by a menacing letter of
dismissal from Mr. Robinson, forbidding Branwell the
premises. According to Branwell (as he wrote a friend) it
contained a threat to shoot him.

The wearisomely repetitive phases of the Branwell-Mrs.
Robinson drama began with a state of mind which Branwell described to a friend: "I have lain during nine long weeks
utterly shattered in body and broken down in mind."

Its various stages were marked by liquor-stupefied days;
drunken, suicide-raving nights; agonized self-recrimination
and remorse; bitter self-reproach; incessant money-wheedling
for drink and drugs; court summonses and sheriff's calls at
the parsonage, initiated by Bradford and Halifax unpaid pub-
keepers; and a melodramatization of his self-martyrdom. In
Branwell's letters to the two main recipients of his agoniz-
ings, Grundy and Leyland, he expressed his torment both
verbally and in pen-drawings, in, for example, phrases
describing himself as "roasting daily and nightly over a slow
fire," and in drawings of himself tied to a burning stake or
strung up ready for hanging.

Like an ordinary theatrical tragedy, the love-drama (which
was partly paralleled by Emily in her novel and by Anne
in *The Tenant of Wildfell Hall*) had three main phases.
During the first period, immediately after his dismissal,
Branwell retained a measure of hope. It was based on the
elderly, invalidish Mr. Robinson's approaching death, when
Branwell envisioned, in his own words, "falling heir to the
lady and her estates." In this phase Branwell, while on a recuperative trip to Liverpool with his friend, John Brown,
imagined that "wherever I went a certain woman robed in
black, calling herself 'Misery' walked by my side."

He wrote a poem, which was published under a pseudonym

in the *Halifax Guardian*, designed to communicate his passion to Mrs. Robinson. He undertook two major literary projects, the writing of a three volume novel and a long, narrative poem entitled "Morely Hall," dedicated to his friend Leyland, on the theme of the latter's ancestral estate. About six weeks after his return from Liverpool, he started writing the novel's first volume. He was motivated partly by a desire, as he wrote, to "wile away my torment," and partly as a quick, easy means of at last attaining the literary renown for which he had so long hungered. He believed that "a novel is the most saleable article." He added, with a touch of his former literary bravado,

> . . . so that where ten pounds would be offered for a work which would require the utmost stretch of a man's intellect, 200 pounds would be a refused offer for three volumes whose composition would require the smoking of a cigar and the humming of a tune.

And even more grandiosely, comparing himself to Shakespeare, Smollett and Fielding:

> My novel is the result of years of thought and if it records as faithfully as the pages in Hamlet or Lear, the conflicting feelings and clashing pursuits in our uncertain path through life, I shall be as much gratified as if I had leapt from the present bathos of fictitious literature on to the firmly fixed rock honoured by the foot of a Smollett or a Fielding.

A year later, on May 25th, 1846, Mr. Robinson died and the drama's second phase, when Branwell's passion, at least so he believed, would inevitably be consummated, began. But instead, he was assailed by messages from Mrs. Robinson (brought by her coachman) and by notes from the lady's doctor and her maid, a Miss Anne Marshall, telling him, as he wrote a friend, that "his concealed hopes must be given up."

In Branwell's version (in his explanations to his two friends), Mr. Robinson's will had forbidden Mrs. Robinson further relations with Branwell. But either Branwell had been intentionally misinformed or he was deluding himself. When Mr. Robinson's will was later probated, it had no such clause. Furthermore, Mrs. Robinson was undergoing what would now be recognized as a nervous breakdown, from which her doctor believed she would not recover. Mrs. Robinson's mental disorder had been, apparently, caused by a remorseful feeling of responsibility for her husband's death and for Branwell's present dejection.

Branwell, describing the lady's state of mind to Leyland, writes:

> . . . her horror at having been the first to delude me into a state of wretchedness and her agony at having been the cause of her husband's death . . . (with the result that) her sensitive mind is totally wrecked . . . she wandered into talk of entering a nunnery and the doctor fairly debars me from hope.

Branwell's emotions may be imagined. Charlotte, describing Branwell's mood about a month after Mr. Robinson's death, writes:

> The death of Mr. Robinson served Branwell for a pretext to throw all about him into a hubbub and confusion with his emotions. And when he heard that Mr. Robinson had altered his will to prevent all chances of a marriage between his widow and Branwell, he then became intolerable. To Papa he allows rest neither day or night. Branwell declares that he neither can nor will do anything for himself; good situations have been offered him but he will do nothing but drink and make us all wretched.

Branwell writes even more melodramatically:

It is hard work. I would bear it, but my health is so bad that the body seems as if it could not endure the mental shock. My appetite is lost; nights are dreadful. I could be glad if God would take me. In the next world, I could not be worse than I am in this . . . A misery that has only one black end . . . for four nights I have not slept, for three days I have not tasted food.

In his various rationalizations, Branwell envisioned his lady (with typically paranoic self-delusion) as being forcibly restrained by his enemies: her relatives and estate trustees who, he wrote, "hate me like Hell." At one point Branwell, with no basis in fact, writes:

The executing trustees detest me and one declares that if he sees me he will shoot me. . . . her relatives who controlled the whole property overwhelm her . . . she has been terrified by vows which she was forced to swear to, on her husband's deathbed . . . a complete severance from him in whom lay her whole heart's feelings (and) she has succumbed in terror.

Mrs. Robinson's supposed, according to Branwell, "insanity" was certainly one of his self-deceptions. For in the drama's third and final stage, which occurred during the early summer of 1848, Mrs. Robinson had recovered sufficiently (as her two daughters told Anne when they visited the parsonage) to be calmly awaiting the death of the wife of Sir Edward Scott in order to marry him (which she later did, as Charlotte reported to Ellen).

Through the mirage of deception created both by Branwell's delusions and by Mrs. Robinson in her messages to Branwell, the entire truth is nearly undetectable. Yet tiny bits of authentic evidence do imply at least a germ of truth in Branwell's claim that there were emotional ties between himself and Mrs. Robinson. According to the most reliable source and the only witness actually present, Anne believed that, as noted above, "there was something between them." Certainly, it was not in Anne's nature, or in her pious Methodist principles, to lie. She characterized Mrs. Robinson as "a mixture of weakness, deceit and perverseness." Charlotte described Mrs. Robinson to Ellen as follows: "A worse woman, I believe, hardly exists; the more I hear of her, the more deeply she revolts me."

Hence (even allowing for the natural prejudice of Branwell's two sisters), from Mrs. Robinson's own behavior it certainly was in character for her to deceive her husband and later deny her relations with Branwell. She sued Mrs. Gaskell for the latter's description of the affair in her *Life of Charlotte Bronte*.

The core of the truth, as one pieces together the scant, reliable evidence, was probably that Mrs. Robinson, the bored young wife of a dying man, had been sufficiently diverted by Branwell, her son's handsome tutor, seventeen years younger, who even in his disintegration remained a fascinating companion, and entered into some degree of intimacy with him. Branwell's words, "daily pleasure chastised by fear for four years" are ambiguous about the exact nature of their sexual relations. But whatever the truth, certainly, when Mrs. Robinson became a wealthy widow (she literally forced one of her daughters into a mercenary marriage, according to Anne's statement), a penniless, unstable, drunken, unknown writer-artist was a person merely to be rid of, which Mrs. Robinson did.

Certainly to Branwell, his lady represented a final (in Charlotte's phrase) "polar star of hope." Perhaps a miraculous reprieve for a misspent life, she represented (in Branwell's words) "a being worthy of all love and who for years has given him all love" and even more important, represented the financial security which he believed had so long hindered him, as a writer, and would now free him from drudgery. He wrote to a friend that Mrs. Robinson was

> A lady with whom, in more than competence, I might live at leisure to try to make a name for myself in posterity, without being pestered by the small and countless botherments, which like mosquitos sting me in the world of workday toil. That hope, and herself, are gone. She to wither into patiently pining decline. I to make room for drudgery on one ill-fitted to bear it.

Actually, these mixed motives which Branwell's words imply, even more than his self-pitying, drunken protestations and self-martyrdom, endow the drama with its note of bathos and real undignity and, furthermore, cast a doubt on the authenticity of Branwell's self-described, undying passion.

But, however unrealistic his hope or dubious his motives, henceforth he was doomed both as a human being and as a creative artist. Perhaps, the most poignant, because the most deeply felt, and hence the truest of his various self-descriptions during this period, was his lament for the death of his talent. Writing to Leyland in January, 1847, he says:

> Noble writings, works of art, music or poetry now, instead of rousing my imagination, cause a whirlwind of blighting sorrow that sweeps over my mind with unspeakable dreariness, and if I sit down and try to write, all ideas that used to come in sunlight now press round me in funeral black; for nearly every pleasurable excitement has changed to insipidity or pain. And I used to think that if I could have for a week the free range of the British Museum, the library included, I could feel as though I were placed for seven days in Paradise, but now, really, my eyes could roam over the Elgin Marbles, the Egyptian salon and the more treasured volumes like the eyes of a dead codfish.

Neither of his two former remedies for despair—alcohol

and his Haworth friends—now brought him the faintest comfort. If, as he wrote in one of his letters, "wine drives off their cares, such cures only make me outwardly passable in company, but never drive off mine." His torment was further increased by his belief that his family were utterly unable to "understand the nature of my sufferings."

Indeed, Branwell had now become, in the Brontes' lives, as Charlotte wrote about her own feelings, "an impediment to all happiness." She, at least, had reached a state of mind in which she viewed him not only with undisguised contempt but even hatred. On one occasion she had to force herself to even speak to him. As she wrote to Ellen, "It was very forced work to address him."

Despite Ellen's long intimacy with the Brontes, Charlotte refused to permit a visit from Ellen in Branwell's present phase. She wrote Ellen: "While he is here you shall not come. I am more confirmed in that resolution the more I see of him. I wish I could say one word to you in his favor. But I cannot."

As Branwell's tragedy progressed, one has the impression that he symbolized to his sisters, even if unconsciously, their own various defeats. Certainly, beneath Charlotte's bitter attitude, one feels that she held him partly responsible for her own difficulties. Charlotte at thirty, although in reality her literary career was beginning, feared that she was dying creatively, that her literary hopes were doomed. She writes to Ellen in the autumn, 1845: "My life is passing away and I am doing nothing, earning nothing, but I see no way out of the mist." Again, early the next year, in March 1846, to Ellen: "I shall be thirty-one my next birthday, my youth is gone like a dream, and very little use have I ever made of it. What have I done these last thirty years? Precious little."

More realistically, Branwell had now become a serious hindrance at the parsonage. His pub debts were a constant drain on the Brontes' limited means. In December 1846 Charlotte related to Ellen an incident which recurred: ". . . the arrival of a Sheriff's officer on a visit to Branwell inviting him either to pay his debts or take a trip to York. Of course, his debts had to be paid. It is not agreeable to lose money time after time in this way."

The Brontes' inept handling of Branwell in his present mood, doubtless one of a long series of such misunderstandings, and the width of the estrangement between him and at least one Bronte, Charlotte, is clearly visible in a tiny episode in which Branwell made a touching gesture of repentance and reform. Emily was, one imagines, more understanding. But, unfortunately, her behavior is not recorded. Branwell had read psalms and hymns to an ailing Parish child and had then recounted the incident to Charlotte. He writes:

> I came away with a heavy heart, for I felt sure she would die, and went straight home, where I fell into melancholy musings. I wanted somebody to cheer me. I often do; but no kind word finds its way to my ears. Charlotte observed my depression and asked what ailed me. So I told her. She looked at me with a look which I shall never forget if I live to be a hundred years. It was not like her at all. It wounded me as if someone had struck me a blow on the mouth. It involved ever so many things in it. It was a dubious look, as if I had been a wild beast. And then came the baffled, painful expression which was worse than all. It said: "I wonder if that's true?" But as she left the room, she seemed to accuse herself of having wronged me and said: "She is my little scholar and I will go and see her." I replied not a word. I was too much cut up. I came over to the Black Bull and made a night of it, in sheer disgust and desperation. Why could not they give me some credit where I was trying to be good?

Anne reacted, inevitably, in religious terms to Branwell's tragedy. Her emotions were those of a dedicated martyr. She was moved to devote the theme of her second novel to what Charlotte described as "the terrible effects of talents misused and facilities abused." Even though this theme was deeply repugnant, "she hated her work but would pursue it. Hers was a naturally sensitive, reserved and dejected nature. What she saw sank deeply into her mind. It did her harm. She brooded over it until she believed it a duty to reproduce every detail as a warning to others."

But to Emily, who had long foreseen and predicted, in her poems, Branwell's tragic end, its actual denouement—his disastrous love for Mrs. Robinson—though certainly a source of emotional misery, must have seemed an anti-climax. In Emily's only subsequent reference to Branwell she characterized him, with a mildness which seems a miracle of understatement, as "a hopeless being" (as Charlotte quoted Emily in a letter in March 1846).

The true significance of the Branwell-Mrs. Robinson drama to Emily was in providing her with timely material for a novel. It gave her an external framework for a theme on which she had long brooded—the theme of many of her poems—sinful love. The resemblances between the real-life Branwell-Mrs. Robinson episode and the plot of Emily's novel (the writing paralleled Branwell's affair in time) are too numerous to trace in detail. But a central core of similarity is indisputable, primarily in subject matter. Emily's novel (like Branwell's love-drama) deals with a tragedy created by a repressed, illegitimate passion. In the novel the passion's object is a married foster-sister, the elder Cathy; in real-life it is a married lady, Mrs. Robinson. The Heathcliff-Branwell lover is a borderline case, obsessed, driven mad, by frustration. True, Emily had explored the theme of sinful love in poems, long before Branwell's love-debacle. But not until *Wuthering Heights* did she deal with it in a full-length narrative about real people.

Secondly, there is the resemblance in characterization.

Heathcliff and Cathy are, in certain phases (with aspects of Emily's own nature mixed in), nearly identical to Branwell and Mrs. Robinson. Heathcliff, like Branwell, is a doomed evil-doer, maniacally driven by unrequited passion. Like the elder Cathy, when Mrs. Edgar Linton of Thrushcross Grange, Mrs. Robinson is rich, mercenary, prideful, perverse, desperately entangled in and, in fact, nervously broken by an unlawful passion. Certainly, Mrs. Robinson (when her doctor wrote to Branwell, in Branwell's words, "her mind was wrecked. She wandered into talk of entering a nunnery") was temporarily as mentally deranged as Cathy in her pre-death mental illness. One remembers the novel's magnificent scene when Cathy Linton, on her deathbed at Thrushcross Grange, in her delirium is no longer able to repress both her yearning for Heathcliff and her native moorland. She tears up her bedpillow and identifies the feathers, to Nelly Dean, as belonging to remembered moorland birds. Nelly Dean tells Lockwood:

> Tossing about, she increased her feverish bewilderment to madness. She seemed to find childish diversion in pulling the feathers and tore the pillow with her teeth . . . and ranging them on the sheet according to their different species: Her mind strayed to other associations. "That's a turkey's and this is a wild duck's; this is a pigeon's. Ah, they put pigeon's feathers in the pillows. No wonder I could not die! And here is a moor cock's; and this, I should know it among thousands . . . it's a lapwing's. Bonny bird, wheeling over our heads in the middle of the moor. It wanted to get to its nest, for the clouds had touched the swells, and it felt rain coming. This feather was picked up from the heath, the bird was not shot; we saw its nest in winger full of little skeletons. Heathcliff set a trap over it and the old ones dare not come. I made him promise he'd

never shoot a lapwing after that and he didn't. Yes, here are more! Did he shoot my lapwings, Nelly?"

Branwell's drunken ravings about his lady's imagined "insanity" (in his letters) were probably not unlike Cathy's delirium in *Wuthering Heights*.

Thirdly, there is the similarity in physical background. The contrast between Thorp Green and Haworth Parsonage provided Emily with an effective dramatic juxtaposition. The contrast between bare, stark Wuthering Heights farm (like the parsonage in this respect) where Heathcliff suffers in mental exile and solitude (again like Branwell in Haworth) and the very different reality and vision always present in both Branwell's and Heathcliff's minds of luxurious, beservanted Thrushcross Grange-Thorp Green vividly dramatizes their anguish.

Yet, if elements in Emily's novel resemble Branwell's love affair, the novel's underlying theme had implications far beyond the limited and sordid Robinson episode. Essentially, the Robinson drama is merely that of a mercenary, selfish and emotionally dishonest lady, disentangling herself from an undesirable love affair with her son's tutor. Indeed, one feels that the emotional tone of Heathcliff's and Cathy's love was probably more akin to the early bond between Emily and Branwell. It seems to the present writer that the much debated relevance of the Robinson drama to *Wuthering Heights* was mainly in furnishing Emily with dramatic material.

Within a few months after the first outbreak of Branwell's drama, Emily began writing her novel. The noted Bronte authority, Miss F. E. Ratchford, believes that *Wuthering Heights* was begun in the autumn of 1845. Theories which base fictional creations on real events can be misleading. Yet it seems incredible that Emily's novel was not influenced by this similar melodrama being enacted in the parsonage, as she was writing her novel (in her tiny, box-bedroom and in the parsonage garden on her folding, rosewood desk) and revising it during the nightly discussions with her two sisters in the parsonage dining-living-room.

14

EMILY'S POEMS AND
WUTHERING HEIGHTS
ARE PUBLISHED

Despite Emily's ready made material, Emily would probably never have written *Wuthering Heights* had it not been for Charlotte. Charlotte was a moving force behind the fact that Emily abandoned her Gondal tales to write a modern novel. Emily wrote *Wuthering Heights* as a direct result of the printing of her poems in a joint book of verse by the three sisters, which was entirely Charlotte's doing.

When Charlotte had accidentally discovered one of Emily's two poetry notebooks in the fall of 1845, she had persuaded Emily to agree to their publication in a joint book of poems by the three sisters. When the poems appeared or a few months earlier, Emily had *then* decided to write a novel. As Charlotte recalled, in describing the stimulating effect of the sisters' first appearance in print:

> The mere effort to succeed had given a wonderful zest to existence, it must be pursued. We each set to work on a prose tale; Ellis Bell produced Wuthering Heights, Acton Bell, Agnes Grey, and Currer Bell also wrote a narrative in one volume.

Certainly, Emily's poems would have remained unpublished, like Emily Dickinson's, at least during her lifetime, had it not been for Charlotte. According to Charlotte, Emily had neither the desire nor the practical initiative to make the necessary, rather complicated publishing arrangements. Emily was afflicted by that peculiarity of the literary mind, particularly the original mind, an almost morbid uncertainty about her own very great talents. As Charlotte recalled, in describing her ordeal in overcoming Emily's natural diffidence, "It took days to persuade her that such poems merited publication." And Emily entirely lacked Charlotte's ability to deal successfully with the outside world. As Charlotte very truly explained:

> An interpreter ought always to have stood between her and the world. Emily had no worldly wisdom. Her powers were unadapted to the practical business of life; she would fail to defend her manifest right; to consult her legitimate advantage.

Charlotte has movingly chronicled her intense emotions, the Autumn day of 1845, when she chanced to read Emily's poems, and her difficulties in combating Emily's anger and refusal to have her poems published:

> One day in the Autumn of 1845, I accidentally lighted on a manuscript volume of verse in my sister Emily's handwriting. Of course, I was not surprised knowing that she could and did write verses. I had a deep conviction that they were not common effusions; not at all like the poetry women generally write. To my ear they had a music, wild, melancholy, elevating.

And to her later friend and editor, Mr. Williams, Charlotte wrote:

> I know of no woman who ever lived who wrote such poetry before. Condensed energy, clearness, finish— strange, strong pathos are their characteristics; utterly dif-

ferent from the usual diffusiveness; the laboured yet most
feeble wordiness, which dilutes the writing of even the
most popular poetesses. That is my deliberate and quite
impartial opinion. Of its startling excellence I am deeply
convinced and have been from the first moment. The pieces
are short but they are very genuine; they stirred the heart
like the sound of a trumpet when I read them alone and in
secret.

And, believing that

such poems merited publication . . . the deep excitement
I felt forced from me the confession of the discovery I
had made.

But:

I was sternly rated for having taken an unwarranted
liberty . . . the recesses of whose mind and feelings even
the nearest and dearest could with impunity intrude un-
licensed.

It took hours to reconcile her to the discovery I had
made and days to persuade her that such poems merited
publication. But I knew that a mind like hers could not be
without some spark of honourable ambition and refused
to be discouraged in my attempt to fan the flame. By dint
of entreaty and reason, I at last wrung out a reluctant con-
sent.

Meanwhile, Anne, who had already published a few poems,
anonymously,

. . . quietly produced some of her own compositions, in-
timating that since Emily's gave me pleasure, I might like
to look at hers. I could not but be a partial judge. Yet I
thought these verses too had a sweet, sincere pathos of their
own. We agreed to arrange a small selection of poems and
if possible to get them published.

Yet, interestingly, when Emily finally agreed, she withheld her personal love poems. None of these were included in the twenty-one poems which each of the sisters contributed to the book. Several of Emily's finest poems, although they were already written, were omitted. Emily was probably consciously hiding the identity of her love which again underlines the role of Barnwell in her love poems.

In contrast to Emily's practical ineptitude, Charlotte (perhaps with some suggestions from her two sisters) handled the publication details with skilled professionalism. Charlotte has explained her initial difficulty in even getting a reply from publishers to her letters about the poems. Evidently London publishers were not easily accessible to unknown poets writing from a remote, county parsonage. Charlotte later remembered gratefully the kind advice of an Edinburgh firm, Messrs. Chambers, who had written to suggest a London firm, Aylott and Jones, of Paternoster Row. As she recalled:

> The great puzzle lay in getting answers from the publishers. Being greatly harassed, I ventured to apply to an Edinburgh firm, Messrs. Chambers. THEY may have forgotten but I have not. I received a brief and businesslike reply, on which we acted and at last made our way.

In early January 1846, Aylott and Jones, religious and classical booksellers, agreed to publish the poems for the sum of thirty-one pounds for a first edition. Charlotte's letters to Aylott and Jones during the next few months were filled with minute instructions about the book: type to be used, quality of paper, the magazines in which to advertise and to which review copies should be sent, etc. In one of her letters she instructs that the book be

> . . . printed in one octave volume of the same quality of paper and type as Moxon's last edition of Wordsworth . . .

somewhat reduced though still clear type, not too small and good paper . . . neatly done up in cloth . . .

and, directing that two pounds be spent on advertisements, she listed various magazines to which review copies and advertisements were to be sent. And

> . . . any other periodicals to which you have been in the habit of sending copies. Those I have mentioned will suffice for advertising. The success of a work depends more on the notices than on the quantity of advertisements.

Apparently, Aylott and Jones fulfilled Charlotte's requests meticulously. The only note of discord between Charlotte and her publishers was a minor complaint about a proof error. When the sisters discovered an error: "Tumbling stars instead of trembling stars, which would throw an air of absurdity over the whole poem," as Charlotte explained, she demanded that "all proofs be sent to us in turn." Oddly, the Brontes had no copy of their original manuscript. Charlotte added that they could correct their proofs from memory.

When the little volume of Bronte poems finally appeared on May 2nd (under the famous Bronte pseudonym of Bell, to avoid the "prejudice" against "Authoresses," as Charlotte explained), it was, as Charlotte wrote, "a drug" and "scarcely known." Yet its failure and sale of only two copies did not disturb Charlotte's passionate belief in Emily as a poet, even though she described it caustically in letters which she sent to half a dozen leading writers with presentation copies. Writing to Thomas De Quincey about a year and a half later, in January 1847, she stated:

> My relatives, Ellis and Acton Bell and myself heedless of the repeated warnings of various respectable publishers have committed the rash act of printing a volume of poems.

The consequences have, of course, overtaken us. Our book is found to be a drug. No man needs it or heeds it. In a year our publisher has disposed of but two copies, and by what painful efforts he has succeeded in getting rid of these two, himself only knows.

We have decided on distributing, as presents, a few copies of what we cannot sell . . .

Charlotte had too much literary intelligence and objectivity not to realize her own limitations as a poet. As she recognized, quite rightly:

All that merits to be known are the poems of Ellis Bell. The fixed conviction I held, and hold, of the worth of these poems has not received the confirmation of much favorable criticism; but I must retain it notwithstanding.

Emily probably felt otherwise. Emily had less rapport with and knowledge of the real world. Perhaps, more emotional in her hopes, it was probably a bitter disappointment. Actually, however, the poems had excellent reviews in three leading literary magazines, one of whose critics perceived the importance of Emily's poems. The Athaneum's reviewer had written:

A family in whom the instinct of song . . . rising in that of Ellis Bell into an inspiration which may yet find an audience in the outer world. A fine, quaint spirit which may yet have things to speak that men will be glad to hear and an evident power of wing which may reach the heights, not here attempted.

But, on the whole, Emily, like Charlotte, evidently thought of the book as a failure. Charlotte, writing of the sisters' refusal to be defeated, said: "Ill success failed to crush us." Evidently, the good reviews did not offset Emily's original doubts. Charlotte, writing to her editorial friend, Mr. Williams, about Emily and her poems, said: "The author never alludes to them and when she does it is with scorn."

If the publication of her poems was, one gathers, a disappointment to Emily, that of *Wuthering Heights* must have been a heart-rending experience. It had misunderstanding, derogatory reviews; extremely unfortunate publishing auspices. It was so entirely overshadowed by Charlotte's critically acclaimed, best-selling *Jane Eyre*, that Emily's novel was thought, in Charlotte's words, merely "an earlier, ruder work by the author of *Jane Eyre*."

Unfortunately, we have no direct clue to Emily's feelings. But Charlotte's comments about the book's fate probably reflects Emily's disillusion. Charlotte writes:

> Critics failed to do justice. The immature but very real powers of *Wuthering Heights* were scarcely recognized; its import and nature were misunderstood; the identity of its author was misrepresented. It was said this was an earlier, ruder attempt by the pen which had produced *Jane Eyre*.

Wuthering Heights, written during the long and particularly bleak winter of 1845-46, in between attacks of flu and Branwell's drunken bouts, was finally published in December of 1847, after about a year and a half of rejections, according to Charlotte. All the circumstances of its publication were, almost dramatically, weighted toward its failure and its being entirely eclipsed by Charlotte's *Jane Eyre*.

Jane Eyre was published by one of London's most distinguished publishers, Smith, Elder. They believed it to be a great novel. The firm's senior reader, Mr. Williams, who later became Charlotte's friend, had highly recommended it to Mr. George Smith. The latter had been so impressed by the opening pages that he had cancelled his week-end plans to read it uninterruptedly. Famous overnight, Charlotte had been instantly acclaimed by such literary giants as Thackeray and George Henry Lewes, among others.

But, unfortunately, Emily's (and Anne's) publisher, Mr. T. C. Newby, Mortimer Street, London, was not only financially dishonest but morally irresponsible. *Wuthering Heights* was published under a cloud of crooked financial maneuverings; publication delays; intentional falsification of Emily's identity and typographical errors. Emily and Anne had agreed to pay Mr. Newby one-half of the book's publishing expenses—fifty pounds for the first edition of 350 copies. The money was to be returned when the edition sold. Mr. Newby never repaid his debt. Charlotte was still trying to collect it after her two sisters' deaths. Furthermore, as Charlotte wrote, the "manuscripts" were criminally "neglected" by Mr. Newby. He subjected the authors to "exhausting delays."

Probably Mr. Newby finally decided to publish *Wuthering Heights* only because of *Jane Eyre*'s success. *Wuthering Heights* was in proof in early August, 1847, and it was still unpublished in October when *Jane Eyre* appeared. Mr. Newby's advertisements of *Wuthering Heights* were not only, in Charlotte's words, "scant and rare," but they were deliberately worded to suggest that Ellis Bell was really Currer Bell, which distressed Emily. As Charlotte wrote, "Ellis disdains such trickery." Although Emily corrected the proofs of *Wuthering Heights*, it was printed with the original errors. Miraculously the book sold fairly well.

Unhappily, *Wuthering Heights* was not recognized as a great novel until two years after Emily's death. Sydney Dobell, writing in *The Palladium Magazine* in 1850, was the first critic to perceive that *Wuthering Heights* was a greater work than *Jane Eyre*. In his essay, he described the author of *Wuthering Heights* (whom ironically he believed to be Charlotte) as a "genius" and the novel as a work of "unconscious

but exquisite art." But during Emily's lifetime only two critics had not dismissed *Wuthering Heights* as a "powerful" but
"shocking picture of the worst forms of humanity," as one
reviewer wrote. Of the two good reviews, one rated *Wuthering Heights* as inferior to *Jane Eyre*. The reviewer in *Douglas
Jerrold's Magazine* had said of Emily: "The writer of Wuthering Heights wants but skill to make a great artist." But in
the other favorable review, in *The Atlas Magazine*, the critic
had written: "The work of Currer Bell is a great perform-
ance; that of Ellis Bell is only a promise but it is a colossal
one."

Just as Emily was unequipped to deal with Mr. Newby's
dishonesty, she was, according to Charlotte, psychologically
unprepared for the reviews. According to Charlotte, Emily
was far too close to her Yorkshire material to realize not
only that it was unusual but that it would shock the Victorian mind. As Charlotte rightly perceived:

> To strangers unacquainted with the locality . . . *Wuth-
> ering Heights* must appear a rude and strange production
> . . . Men and women will hardly know what to make of
> the rough, rude utterance, the harshly manifested passions,
> the unbridled aversion of unlettered moorland minds. . . .
> Her imagination was a trifle more sombre than sunny
> . . . wrought creations like Heathcliff, like Earnshaw, like
> Catherine. Having formed these beings she knew not what
> she had done. If it was complained that the vivid scenes
> banished sleep and disturbed mental peace, Ellis Bell would
> wonder what was meant and suspect affectation. Her mind
> gathered those tragic and terrible traits in the secret annals
> of every rude vicinage.

Even Charlotte, who personally admired Emily's novel tre-
mendously, wondered: "Whether it is right to create such
beings as Heathcliff. I do not think it is. Heathcliff stands
unredeemed." Yet, unfortunately, Charlotte was more per-

ceptive and farseeing about the quality of *Wuthering Heights* than most of Emily's critics:

> *Wuthering Heights* was hewn in a wild workshop, with simple tools, out of homely materials. He wrought with a rude chisel and from no model but the vision of his own meditations. With time and labour the crag took human shape . . . beautiful for its colouring is of mellow grey, and the moorland grass clothes it, and heath, with its strange blooming fragrance grows faithfully close to the giant's foot.

Emily's disappointment must have been deep. For after Emily's death Charlotte, with belated sensitivity, wrote that: "When critics said it was a ruder work by Currer Bell, we laughed, at first, but I deeply lament it now."

By an odd quirk of temperament, Emily did not share in the only worldly reward from the three novels. When Charlotte and Anne went to London in early July (1848) to iron out Mr. Newby's dishonest sale of the American rights to Anne's second novel as being by Currer Bell, Emily remained in Haworth. Charlotte and Anne, within hours after receiving a letter from Charlotte's publishers, had walked through a summer rainstorm and had entrained for London. Here, they not only revealed their identities to Smith, Elder (in Charlotte's subsequently famous phrase: "we are three sisters") and arranged with Smith, Elder to publish a second edition of the Bronte poems, but under the auspices of Mr. Smith and Mr. Williams they had a brief glimpse of the London literary scene and a taste of literary renown.

But Emily, as Charlotte had previously explained to her publishers probably in resentment, "detested the artificial man of cities." "It (visiting London) is one no power on earth would induce Ellis Bell to avail himself of."

15

DEATH OF EMILY
AND BRANWELL

Emily's "only wreath," as Charlotte described Mr. Dobell's essay, "dropped on a grave." And surely the fact that
Emily died a year after *Wuthering Heights* was published,
December 19th, 1848, and within two months after Branwell
had died, September 24th, could not be entirely by chance.
Emily Bronte's death was complicated by her complex inner
life. Particularly Branwell's death and *Wuthering Heights'*
failure had their effect in breaking her will to live at the
age of thirty. Just as Branwell, whose romantic, dramatic
temperament was in many ways similar to Emily's, died and
admittedly wanted to die when his innermost dream of
marrying Mrs. Robinson could not be realized (and he did
die within a very few months of Mrs. Robinson's re-mar-
riage), certainly Charlotte's account of Emily during her last
illness suggests a similar emotional pattern.

Branwell's death, like his life, was simpler, more easily understandable and more melodramatic than Emily's. Resentment against his sisters' literary achievement, which he had
desired so intensely himself could have been, but actually was
not an added cause. Mercifully, he died unaware that *Jane
Eyre, Wuthering Heights* and *Agnes Grey* had been published. As Charlotte explains:

My unhappy brother never knew what his sisters had done in literature, he was not aware that they had even published a line. We could not tell him for fear of causing him too deep a pang of remorse, for his own time misspent and talents misapplied.

Difficult as it must have been to hide manuscripts at the parsonage, Charlotte probably was accurate. The Brontes had always been incessant writers. During the winter (1845-46) when the novels were written, Branwell was too deeply embedded in his own disintegration and drunkenness for the meaning of publishers' letters, the buying of reams of paper at the local stationers' (who told Mrs. Gaskell that he walked to Bradford for extra supplies for the Brontes), and even the arrival of proofs, to penetrate. For the same reason, Branwell's friends' claims that he wrote either all or a part of Emily's novel are unbelievable. Indeed, these claims have long since been discarded by Bronte biographers.

Branwell Bronte's death was, supposedly, unexpected. Yet in Grundy's description of his last meeting with Branwell— characteristically, a dinner at the Black Bull Inn—Branwell's end must have been obvious for months. Grundy paints a moving portrait of the dying Branwell: his appearance changed almost beyond recognition; the light of insanity in his eyes and death, which he now viewed with equanimity, even hope, in his heart. Grundy describes Branwell a few days before the latter's death:

> His mass of red, unkempt, uncut hair wildly flashing around a great, gaunt forehead, the cheeks yellow and hollow, the mouth fallen, the thin, white lips, not trembling but shaking, the shrunken eyes, once small now glaring with the light of madness . . . after a second glass of brandy, and some dinner, he became something like the Bronte of old. I never knew his intellect clearer. He described himself as waiting anxiously for death, indeed long-

ing for it, and happy, in these, his sane moments, to think
it was so near. He once again declared that death was due
to the story I knew.

His death was preceded by a last-minute, deathbed repentance, a reconciliation to his father's religion. During his last
two days, Charlotte noted in him

. . . the peculiar change which frequently precedes death.
He became gentle and affectionate. His demeanor, his language, his sentiments, were all singularly altered and softened. Towards his family all bitterness seemed gone.

Dying, he joined in Mr. Bronte's prayers and muttered,
"Amen." But his repentance only partly consoled the grief-
stricken Mr. Bronte, who in his desolation, according to
Charlotte, "cried out his loss like David for that of Absalom:
'My son! My son!' and refused, at first, to be comforted."
Charlotte, more sensible, regretted

. . . not his death, but the wreck of a talent, the ruin of
promise, the untimely extinction of what might have been
a burning and shining light. I had aspirations for him once,
long ago; they perished mournfully. There is a bitterness
for his life and death. Under the circumstances, many
would think our loss rather a relief than otherwise. In
truth, we must acknowledge, in all humanity and gratitude,
that God has greatly tempered judgment with mercy.

Yet despite the fact that Emily had always foreseen Branwell's tragic end (the theme of so many of her poems), she
was probably more deeply stricken by its reality than Charlotte. At Branwell's funeral services, Emily caught a probably "psychosomatic" chill. She never again left the parsonage. Almost immediately, during the next few days, she
had all the symptoms of advanced tuberculosis.

Emily's death, as Charlotte has movingly described
it, was a titanic battle of the will between Emily and

Charlotte: Charlotte's fanatical determination to keep Emily alive pitted against Emily's equally strong will *not* to rally her forces to live, at least not as dictated by Charlotte. From her first moments of illness until she was actually dying she immunized herself against Charlotte's ministrations. First, she refused to have a doctor. In Charlotte's words: "She refused medicine; she rejected medical advice; no reasoning or entreaty would induce her to see a doctor." Charlotte wrote to Ellen, October 28th, 1948:

> Emily's cough and cold are very obstinate. I fear she has pain in the chest, and I sometimes catch a shortness in her breathing when she has moved at all quickly. She looks very, very thin and pale. Her reserved nature occasions me great uneasiness of mind. It is useless to question her; you get no answers. It is still more useless to recommend remedies. They are never adopted.

Emily, like Branwell, must have been impelled, if less consciously and for different and more complex reasons, by a death-will. Yet, given Emily's temperament, her motives were mixed. Charlotte, writing to a London doctor for advice, stated:

> Her resolution not to contend against illness being very fixed, she has never consented to lie in bed for a single day. She sits up from seven in the morning till ten at night. All medical aid, she has rejected, insisting that nature must be left to take its course.

Thus Emily's behavior, in addition to being caused by family tensions and conflict, was also an act of spiritual integrity to natural law—a final salute to her inner ideal: Nature and Natural Man.

Emily's death could not have been otherwise. She died as she had lived: "a law unto herself," in Miss Nussey's words. Her "secret power and fire," as Charlotte once wrote, remained undimmed. Stubbornly independent, she not only refused medical care but ordinary family nursing. The very morning of her death she refused help in dressing herself and had insisted upon descending to the parsonage living room to feed her dogs herself. In Charlotte's rather blunt phrase, "she made haste to leave us."

In this intensive struggle, Charlotte's mental agony was perhaps even more acute than Emily's. As she later described her terrible experience:

> Never in all her life had she lingered over any task, and she did not linger now. She sank rapidly. Yet, while physically she perished, she grew stronger than we had yet known her. Day by day, when I saw with what a front she met suffering, I looked on her with an anguish of wonder and love. I have seen nothing like it. But, indeed, I have never seen her parallel in anything. Stronger than a man, simpler than a child, her nature stood alone. The awful point was that while full of ruth for others, on herself she had no pity; the spirit was inexorable to the flesh; from the trembling hand, the faded eyes, the same service was exacted as they had rendered in health. To stand by and witness this and not dare to remonstrate, was a pain no words can render.

Charlotte, writing to Mr. Williams as Emily's disease reached a more serious phase in November, said:

> She is a real stoic in illness; she neither seeks nor will accept sympathy. To put any questions, to offer any aid, is to annoy; she will not yield a step before pain and sickness until forced. You must look on and see her do what she is not fit to do, and not dare to say a word, a painful necessity for those to whom her health and existence are as precious as the life in her veins.

In November, Mr. Williams had written Charlotte to suggest homeopathic treatment. But, on November 22nd, as Charlotte explained:

> I put your most friendly letter in Emily's hands, taking care not to say a word in favor of homeopathy that would not have answered. It is best, usually, to leave her to form her own judgment; not to advocate the side you wish her to favor; if you do, she is sure to lean in the opposite direction, and she will argue herself into non-compliance. Hitherto, she has refused medicine. No entreaty has availed to induce her to see a physician. And now, she says, "Mr. Williams' intention was kind and good, but he was under a delusion. Homeopathy is only another form of quackery."

The next day, November 23rd, Charlotte, though she clung with pitiable tenacity to hope, writes to Ellen:

> If you were to see her now your impression would be that there is no hope. A more hollow, wasted, pallid aspect. The deep, tight cough continues; the breathing after the least exertion is a rapid pant. She absolutely refuses to see a Doctor. She will give no explanation of her feelings, she will scarcely allow her feelings to be alluded to. Our position is, and has been for some weeks, exquisitely painful. More than once I have been forced to boldly regard the terrible event of her loss as possible and even probable. But nature shrinks from such thoughts.

Finally Charlotte, in agonized desperation, consulted a London doctor by letter. Writing to Ellen nine days before Emily died, on December 10th, she says:

> I have endured such tortures of uncertainty, I could endure it no longer. She declares no poisoning doctor shall come near here. I have written an eminent Doctor in London, giving a minute description of her case and requested an opinion.

When the London doctor's letter finally reached Charlotte, it was not only too late, but, as Charlotte wrote Ellen, the very morning of Emily's death: "His opinion was expressed too obscurely to be of use. He sent some medicine which she would not take."

Emily's unique interest in living remained in books. Only a few days before Emily died, Charlotte, in thanking her publishers for a package of books which they had sent to Emily, stated: "The opening of the parcel and the fascination of the books cheered her. Their perusal occupied her."

And Charlotte's reading aloud of a review of the Bell novels in the American magazine, *The North American Review*, caused a glimmering of human, if unhappy, interest. As Charlotte wrote to Ellen:

> Today as Emily appeared a little easier, I read it aloud to her. The North American Review is worth reading. There is no mincing the matter there. What a bad set the Bells must be. What appalling books they must write. As I sat between them at our quiet but melancholy fireside, I studied the two ferocious authors: "Ellis the man of uncommon talents but dogged, brutal, morose," sat leaning back in his easy chair, drawing his impeded breath as best he could and looking piteously pale and wasted. It is not his wont to laugh, but he smiled, half amused half in scorn as he listened.

Emily, even on the eve of her death, listened to Charlotte read aloud an Emerson essay, "until," as Charlotte later wrote to Mr. Williams, "I found she was no longer listening."

"The next day," as Charlotte wrote in one of her versions of Emily's death, "I thought to recommence, but the first glance told me what would happen before nightfall."

Despite Charlotte's reason, she refused to give up hope. She later wrote Ellen that even then she still believed that Emily "might be with us still for some weeks." But the next mid-morning Charlotte is writing to Ellen: "Moments as dark as these I have never known. I pray for God's support to us all. Hitherto he has granted it."

Certainly by noon even Charlotte must have realized that death was very near. When Charlotte returned from Emily's beloved moors, with a single sprig of heather for Emily, she noticed (as she told Mrs. Gaskell) that Emily, evidently not recognizing it, glanced at it with dim, indifferent eyes. Emily did not relent from her isolation and will-to-die— or at least refusal of life—until she was actually dying. A few minutes before she died she lay down on the parsonage sofa and murmured, belatedly, "If you will call a doctor, I will see him now."

But moving as Emily's "Christian, undemonstrative end" was, as Charlotte wrote in her tribute to Emily, not only because she was Emily Bronte but because of its simple dignity, yet one cannot entirely agree with Charlotte that Emily's death was necessarily "an uprooting in the prime of her own day . . . She died in the promise of her own powers . . . a tree in full bearing struck at the root."

Perhaps Charlotte had manuscripts by Emily, which were later destroyed. For Charlotte wrote about the failure of *Wuthering Heights:* "Neither Ellis nor Acton allowed themselves to sink under want of encouragement; energy nerved the one; endurance upheld the other. They were both prepared to try again."

Two letters, one from Mr. Newby to Emily and one from Charlotte to Smith, Elder, mention that Emily had been currently writing a second novel. After her death, an envelope addressed to Ellis Bell in Mr. Newby's handwriting was found in her desk along with half a dozen reviews of *Wuthering Heights*. Folded to fit this envelope was the following letter in Mr. Newby's handwriting:

I shall have great pleasure in making arrangements for

your next novel. I should not hurry its completion. For I think you are quite right not to let it go before the public until you are well satisfied with it, for much depends on your next work. If it be an improvement, you will have established yourself as a first-rate novelist, but if it falls short, the critics will be too apt to say that you have expended your talent on your first novel. I shall therefore have pleasure in accepting it upon the understanding that its completion be in your own time.

During Emily's illness, Charlotte had written to Smith, Elder about Emily's "second work." Writing on November 7th Charlotte had stated:

> Ellis Bell is at present in no condition to trouble himself with the thought either of writing or publishing. Should it please Heaven to restore his strength and health, he reserves the right of deciding whether or not Mr. Newby has forfeited every claim to his second work.

Perhaps Emily was writing a second novel when she died. But, with a writer whose work was so profoundly rooted in personal experience as Emily Bronte, one wonders from what new experience it could have been derived. Certainly she had depicted in her first novel the central emotional dilemma of her life: the Branwell-Heathcliff-Emily-Cathy emotional vortex. Unless her personal life had drastically altered where would she have found new material?

Yet Emily's early death was, perhaps, less tragic than those hidden aspects of her own life which, in certain phases, had caused her to describe death in her poems as a "rewarding destiny" and to long for the peace of "Eternity."

In the end of *Wuthering Heights*, she had envisaged Heathcliff and Cathy (with perhaps aspects of herself and Branwell in mind, in their destined graves under the Haworth Church stone floor) as at peace in their moorland graves, with, in her novel's magnificent final words: "the soft wind breathing through the grass." Yet, it seems inconceivable to imagine any one of the Brontes, those unquiet spirits, as permanently at peace—even in Eternity.

CRITICAL SUMMARY

Part 1

The Romantic Movement and Wuthering Heights

M~R.~ E~DMUND~ W~ILSON~, the distinguished literary critic, in paraphrasing a statement by the European scholar, Signor de la Praz, in his book, *The Romantic Agony*, has brilliantly defined the Romantic Movement as:

> Romanticism and the Art for Art's Sake Movement represent the attempts of a Europe that had lost its old system of Church and State, based on Divine Authority, to arrive at a new code of conduct based on the human individual.

On the tide of the eighteenth and nineteenth century democratic revolution in Western Europe and the vast social and political upheavals which inaugurated a new phase in Western culture, there had been a revaluation of man, himself. As human reliance on "Divine Authority," in Mr. Wilson's phrase, faltered, the individual and his personal values were stressed. Romanticism expressed this new approach.

For as traditional ideals had declined, it had been necessary to replace these by new spiritual and moral ethics for salvation. Spiritually, man turned inwards to evolve his own personal mystique. In literature this psychic revolution was a new emphasis on the individual, i.e., Romanticism.

The Romantic poets, founders of Romanticism at the turn of the century, by whom Emily was most influenced, had sought their own mystique outside of orthodox religion.

Thus, Wordsworth had evolved a kind of nature mysticism; Keats and Shelley had idealized a sensuous, almost Epicurean, aestheticism. Byron had glorified the Romantic act—Byronism.

In the novel the ideas of the Romantic Movement permeated more slowly. The pre-Romantic novelists, the Brontes' predecessors, Fielding, Smollett and Richardson, had dealt with the ordinary man rather than with the complex individual. Jane Austen, writing a few decades later, had delineated her characters with a new realism. But her characters were still types.

But it remained for the Brontes, these isolated moorland novelists, largely nourished on the Romantic poets, to bring the individual and his inner emotional complexities into the English novel. *Wuthering Heights* has been rated, I believe rightly, as the first major expression of the Romantic Movement in the English novel.

In *Wuthering Heights*, Emily, as I hope to demonstrate, is almost solely concerned with her protagonists' inner lives —their highly individual emotions and beliefs, and her own personal evaluations of their lives. It seems to me that in this respect even more than in its emphasis on Nature that *Wuthering Heights* reveals the influence of the Romantic poets, and is, indeed, an expression of the values of the Romantic Movement. It was a break with tradition whose repercussions were so revolutionary and far-reaching that it still resounds today. For the same reasons which made *Wuthering Heights* the first Romantic novel also made it the forerunner of the modern psychological novel, which penetrates ever more deeply into the human consciousness. And in the twentieth century, with such stream-consciousness novelists as Proust, Virginia Woolf and James Joyce explored the hidden underground of semi- and even sub-conscious states of mind to unearth and evaluate the meaning of formerly invisible aspects of the human mind and personality.

Thus Emily, in *Wuthering Heights*, delves into character motivations. Heathcliff and Cathy: are they good or evil; moral or unmoral? For example, a minor point, take Heathcliff's boyhood moroseness. Is his "inward and outward repulsiveness" due merely to his harsh rearing, or is he innately doomed? When the elder Cathy discards him as dirty, ill-mannered, uneducated for her new friends, the rich gently-bred young Lintons, Heathcliff retires to brood in solitary misery on the moors. Yet, when Nelly Dean reclaims him, he grooms himself and becomes newly "cheerful." He says, "Nelly made me decent, I'm going to be good," and "he gradually lost his frown and began to look quite pleasant." He then envies rather than despises the Lintons, "I wish I had light hair and a fair skin and was dressed, and behaved as well, and were going to be rich." One wonders what is the truth about Heathcliff's real nature?

Heathcliff's and Cathy's inner emotions are the novel's prime, even sole, values. Their relation to the real, everyday world, is never dealt with. Indeed, this aspect of their lives is so entirely evaded that the novel often seems fairy tale-like, almost childish. For example, the means by which Heathcliff during his foreign travels has become a rich man. Heathcliff is never described in relation to the real world. Emily is concerned only with Heathcliff's and Cathy's inner emotions and its essence—in brief, their passion.

And the fierce, animal-like passion which irrevocably binds and, in a sense, dooms them—is it a good or an evil force? A criminal love; or, as it seems in the very end of the novel, magnificent? One cannot tell.

During most of the novel, Heathcliff is merely an ugly revenger whose passion for Cathy has turned him into a viciously destructive sadist. He ruins everyone dividing him from Cathy. He destroys Hindley because he had degraded him before Cathy. He seduces Isabella into marriage to brutally mistreat her because she is the sister of Edgar Linton,

whom Cathy married. He brutalizes his own son Linton
Heathcliff, because he is part Linton. Finally, he entices
Cathy's daughter, Cathy Linton, into a tragic marriage with
his dying son, Linton, to imprison and reduce her to quasi-
servant status at Wuthering Heights.

Certainly, Heathcliff's passion is purely destructive, and
Heathcliff himself motivated only by evil. Yet, in the end,
when Heathcliff and Cathy are united in death and at peace,
Emily described them, despite the devastation they have
caused, as sleeping "quiet slumbers." For the final grave scene
ends:

> I lingered round them under that benign sky, watched
> the moths fluttering among the heath and harebells and
> wondered how anyone could ever imagine unquiet slum-
> bers in that quiet earth.

Essentially, Emily's final comment on this passion provides
the key to the novel's theme. Complex as are the issues involved in Heathcliff's and Cathy's long, tortured, and finally,
tragic love-relationship, in the end Emily appears to be
merely stating (and this denouement is in itself Romanticism)
that since their love is a natural force it becomes evil only
when repressed. Heathcliff, denied, becomes evil. Cathy Linton, in her easy, Thrushcross-Grange luxury bought by emotional self-betrayal, becomes perverse, hating and hateful, and
even in the end, vicious in her conduct towards Edgar. She
finally disintegrates mentally and dies as a direct result. One
remembers the magnificent scene of mutual remorse and re-
crimination, when Cathy is dying; Heathcliff accuses her on
her death bed:

> You loved me then, what right had you to leave me?
> What right for the poor fancy you felt for Linton? Be-
> cause misery and degradation and Death, and nothing that
> God or Satan could have inflicted would have parted us;

you of your own free will did it. I have not broken your heart. You have broken it, and in breaking it, you have broken mine.

And Cathy sobs in self defense: "Let me alone, let me alone. If I have done wrong, I am dying for it."

Yet, despite its terrible repercussions, when that love is eventually fulfilled, even though only symbolically, in death, these two previously self-destroyed destroyers find eternal peace. Emily is telling us that man's deep-lying emotions, his instinctive nature, however unreasonable, unrealistic or even amoral (Heathcliff-Cathy's foster-brother-sisterhood casts an equivocal shadow) can be repressed only at tragic peril. Surely, Emily's resolution in her novel also solves her long-drawn-out, emotional uncertainty about Branwell! Certainly Emily is declaring that more essential than reverence for and obedience to purely man-made social values—material riches and poverty (Edgar Linton is rich—Heathcliff whom Cathy really loves is poor originally); marriage vows (Cathy's and Edgar's are repudiated); religious creed (the servant Joseph's Methodism is mainly ridiculed)—is man's inner emotional integrity to his own nature. Finally, it is a nature mystique—a deification of natural forces—essentially akin to that of the Romantic poets.

Part 2

Wuthering Heights

Indeed, it seems to the present writer that the novel's very Romanticism—its depiction of both outward nature (the natural landscape) and inner nature (Man's inner emotions) —is the essence of the novel's enduring greatness.

For *Wuthering Heights* is, perhaps, the most limited of the great novels. In bare outline it is merely a rather incredible, melodramatic, tale about a moorland boy's thwarted passion for his young, fiery-tempered foster-sister. Vast areas of human experience are ignored in the novel.

Its people, except Heathcliff and Cathy, are not particularly interesting or even in some cases, well-drawn. Lockwood, a chance Yorkshire visitor, is mainly a figurehead. There is Nelly Dean, a self-respecting, God-fearing Yorkshire countrywoman; Joseph, a Methodist servant; the elder Earnshaws who appear briefly; their son, Hindley and his wife (she figures dimly); the rather paper-doll-like Lintons, Edgar and Isabella; Linton Heathcliff (Heathcliff's son by Isabella) and Heathcliff and Cathy Earnshaw.

The novel's plot is often not only naively incredible but pure melodrama. In brief outline the Earnshaws, residing at Wuthering Heights with their children, Cathy and Hindley, adopt a foundling, Heathcliff. When the elder Earnshaws die, Hindley reduces Heathcliff to a servant. Cathy, despite her love for Heathcliff, marries wealthy Edgar Linton. Heathcliff angrily disappears, to return years later, mysteriously rich and travelled.

He buys Wuthering Heights, in revenge brutalizes Hindley

and the latter's son, Hareton, and marries Isabella Linton. Cathy dies in giving birth to her daughter, Cathy. Heathcliff subsequently entices the younger Cathy Linton into marrying his weakling son, Linton Heathcliff. Linton dies and Cathy transfers her affections to Hareton. Heathcliff is eventually reunited to Cathy in death. But let us indicate a few of the novel's glaring deficiencies in plot and in characterization:

How can Heathcliff psychically dominate and imprison Isabella, the younger Cathy, Hindley, and Hareton at Wuthering Heights? Heathcliff and Isabella's twilight, on-horseback elopement resembles an abduction in a melodrama. Cathy Linton's being drawn to Wuthering Heights and entrapped by Heathcliff into marrying his son is not quite credible, nor is her later total enslavement by Heathcliff. The sadistic battles between Heathcliff and Hindley would be edited out of the average novel. Heathcliff peers through a window, his teeth "gleaming" or, in another scene, "crushing his nails into his palms and grinding his teeth." Hareton, when a baby, is in danger of being "dashed against the wall" by his father, Hindley. Hindley menaces Nelly Dean. "He held the knife in his hand and pushed its point between my teeth."

The characters are often caricatures! Heathcliff, during most of the novel, with his fiend's expression and fang-like teeth, is a dime-novel villain. Even Cathy, vividly real as she is, remains (though partly intentionally), almost incredibly a child, particularly when she is married to Edgar. Hindley's degeneration into drunkenness is never clearly motivated. The Lintons, Edgar and Isabella, though they have a core of reality, act mainly as tools of the plot in their easy victimization by Heathcliff and Cathy. Only the minor characters, Nelly Dean and Joseph, remain entirely credible and consistently true.

Nevertheless, the novel remains an immovably fixed peak among great novels. Why?

To repeat, it seems to this writer that the novel's enduring greatness lies in its pure, lyric intensity (even more than its vivid flashes into character) with which it recreates sheer, unadulterated nature; both the natural outward setting and man's inward, deepest-lying emotions, on a plane beyond reason; conventional feeling; temperamental affinities; ordinary, familiar pleasure and pain, joy and sorrow.

Emily Bronte's idea of Heaven is not a Christian Heaven, where the righteous meet a just reward. But it is rather, in her own words, "a glorious world," an Eden-like, natural Paradise, where man is ultimately compensated for earthly, emotional denial and human emotions are at last entirely fulfilled. Cathy, near death, tells Nelly Dean:

> That is not my Heathcliff. I shall love mine yet and take him with me, he's my soul! . . . The thing that irks me most, is this shattered prison, after all. I'm tired of being enclosed here. I'm wearying to escape into that glorious world and to be always there—not seeing it dimly through tears, yearning for it through the walls of an aching heart, but really in it. I shall be incomparably beyond and above you all.

Nelly Dean, describing her death vigil at Cathy's bier, tells Lockwood:

> I am seldom otherwise than happy when watching in the chamber of death. I see a repose that neither Heaven nor Hell can break. I feel an assurance of an endless, shadowless Hereafter, the Eternity they have entered—WHERE LIFE IS BOUNDLESS IN ITS DURATION AND LOVE IN ITS FULLNESS AND JOY IN ITS FULLNESS!

Emily Bronte's delineation of the emotions is profoundly moving because she does not view them in purely personal terms. But rather as irrevocable, torrential, natural forces which resemble, for example, a huge, free-flowing, inland river or a magnificent, primeval crag or waterfall hidden in an impenetrable forest—unharnessable by man. And, for this reason, her dramatic climaxes are so telling.

Rarely, if ever (except, perhaps, in D. H. Lawrence's novels) has the cry of man's inner, emotional disturbance and agony reached us so distinctly, so intensely, so unrestrained by civilized artifices, so in Shakespeare's words "unsicklied o'er by the pale cast of thought." Heathcliff's and Cathy's tragic outcries penetrate our innermost depths, not merely because Heathcliff and Cathy are in themselves moving, but because a great passion is speaking directly through their mouths, indeed almost in spite of them.

When Cathy, weighing the dilemma of her choice between Heathcliff and Edgar Linton, describes the difference in her feelings, she likens her emotions to eternal, natural phenomena. She tells Nelly Dean:

> I cannot express it; but surely you and everybody have a notion that there is or should be an existence beyond joy. What were the use of my creation, if I were entirely contained here? My great miseries in this world have been Heathcliff's miseries; my great thought in living is himself. If all else perished and HE remained, I should still continue to be; and if all else remained, and he were annihilated, the Universe would turn to a mighty stranger; I should not seem part of it.

The essence of her love is described thus:

> My love for Linton, time will change it. I'm well aware as winter changes the trees. My love for Heathcliff resembles the eternal rocks beneath; a source of little visible delight but necessary. Nelly, I am Heathcliff. Whatever our souls are made of—his and mine are the same; and Linton's is as different as a moonbeam from lightning, or frost from fire.

Indeed, the inner emotional reality is so intensely realized that a few evocative words create a mental image, even though that image is not actually described. When Edgar's grave is being dug by the sexton, Heathcliff persuades him to remove the earth from Cathy's grave. Heathcliff opens her coffin. Describing his experience, he tells Nelly Dean, "When I saw her face—IT IS HERS YET—he had hard work to stir me."

With the words "IT IS HERS YET" an unforgettable picture of Cathy's faintly decayed but still clearly recognizable features is immediately imprinted not only in Heathcliff's mind, but miraculously also in the reader's mind.

Heathcliff's and Cathy's passion, from its earliest phases to its tragic end, is enormously heightened by being enacted against a nature background. Actually the love-drama seems to be merely another expression of nature, but in human terms. To use a phrase associated with the French impressionist painters, the drama is enacted "en plein air" on the moorland heights; in the heat of the noon-day mountain sun; under the relentless, driving rain.

For one is made acutely aware of the natural elements: time of day, season, weather, the moorland scene at a certain moment, in a particular light. Invariably, the natural descriptions are interwoven with, and are, a secondary expression of the dramatic action.

Wuthering Heights Farm, psychologically encased in its grim, tragic history, is first presented to the reader in Lockwood's early visit there during an impassable snowstorm; Cathy's love for Linton resembles "the foliage in the woods;" hers for Heathcliff "the eternal rocks beneath." The younger Cathy's and Linton's innocent, spring-time love mood is reflected in their day-dreams of an ideal spring day. Cathy describes Linton's ideal:

A hot, July day lying on a bank of heath in the middle of the moors with the bees humming dreamily among the bloom, and the larks singing high up overhead and the bright sun and blue sky shining steadily and cloudlessly. This was his most perfect idea of Heaven's happiness. Mine was rocking in a rustling green tree, with a wild West wind blowing, and bright clouds flitting rapidly above; and not only larks but throstles, and blackbirds, and linnets and cuckoos pouring out music on every side, and the moors seen at a distance broken into cool, dusky dells; and close by great swells of long grass undulating in waves to the breeze; and woods and sounding water, and the whole world awake and wild with joy. He wanted to lie in an ecstacy of peace; I wanted to sparkle and dance in a glorious jubilee. I said his Heaven would be only half alive; and he said mine would be drunk. At last we agreed to try both as soon as the right weather came.

During the elder Cathy's false convalescence, when she first walks out of doors with Edgar, it is treacherous, disease-breeding March weather. Nelly Dean tells Lockwood, "The first time she left her chamber was in the following March." During their walk, Cathy recreates the March mood when she tells Edgar, "These (flowers) remind me of soft thaw winds, and warm sunshine and early melted snow. Edgar, is there not a South wind? And, is not the snow almost gone?"

When Heathcliff retires to the Grange Park, as Cathy lies dying, he informs Nelly Dean, "I shall be waiting under the larches." The larch trees under which he waits are as real as his misery.

When early next morning Nelly Dean brings him the news of Cathy's death, she realizes that he has stood motionless during the night, as one does, not merely rooted quiet by an impending grief but in the stillness with which one awaits a momentous event, since any previous move would be super-fluous, because of the behavior of nearby animals. In Nelly Dean's words:

He had been standing a long time in that position, for I saw a pair of ousels passing and repassing scarcely three feet from him, busy in building their nest, and regarding his proximity as no more than a piece of timber.

The morning of Cathy's death-travail in giving birth to a new life, young Cathy's, according to Nelly Dean was "bright and cheerful out of doors; stole softened in through the blinds and suffused the couch and its occupant with a mellow, tender glow."

Finally, Heathcliff's death is first hinted when he is menaced by rain. Nelly Dean, glancing at his bedroom window, anxiously notices, "The master's shutter swinging open. He cannot be in bed, I thought, these showers would drench him through with the rain driving straight in."

Unbelievable as it seems that the torrential Heathcliff is really dead, Nelly Dean realizes that it is so, when later, looking at him on his death bed, she sees that the elements have already reached him. She tells Lockwood, "I could not think him dead, but his face and throat were washed with rain."

Certainly, Emily Bronte in her novel, in magnificent language, pronounced one of the great truths of human experience: the ultimate triumph and unalterable nature of passional man. And, in so doing, voiced a message which is continually being discarded, re-discovered, re-buried and re-unearthed. Indeed, our foremost modern poet, T. S. Eliot, in this present, far more complex and spiritually distraught time, though not a Romantic in Emily Bronte's sense, in his *Four Quartets*, in reuniting the individual and his personal fantasies and desires to traditional racial experience, is now again reaffirming it— if for different reasons. One remembers the last few lines of Mr. Eliot's fourth quartet, "Little Gidding":

> And all shall be well and
> All manner of thing shall be well
> When the tongues of flame are in-folded

Into the crowned knot of fire
And the fire and the rose are one.

But Mr. Eliot's very great predecessor, Emily Bronte—perhaps the greatest woman poet, only equaled by Emily Dickinson, and occasionally approached in our own time by Edna St. Vincent Millay—had already prefigured Mr. Eliot's words if in simpler, more elemental terms.

But her great words uttered, let us leave Emily Bronte and her tormented inner complexities and *Wuthering Heights*, with its inequalities.

MATERIALS AND SOURCES

The bulk of the quoted material in this book has been taken from the following books:

Life of Charlotte Bronte, by E. G. Gaskell. Introduction and Notes by Clement Shorter. 1900.

Shakespeare Head Bronte, Their Lives, Friendships and Correspondence, edited by T. J. Wise and J. A. Symington. 1932.

Charlotte Bronte and Her Sisters, by Clement Shorter. 1895.

Charlotte Bronte and Her Circle, by Clement Shorter. 1896.

The Brontes: Lives and Letters, by Clement Shorter. 1908.

The Brontes and Their Circle, by Clement Shorter. 1914.

The Bronte Society Transactions (*see* Bibliography).

Wuthering Heights, by Ellis Bell. Biographical Notice of Ellis and Acton Bell. Editor's Preface by Currer Bell. 1850.

Complete Poems of Emily Bronte, edited by C. W. Hatfield. Introduction by C. W. Hatfield. The Gondal Story by F. E. Ratchford. 1941.

BIBLIOGRAPHY

Books

Bald, Marjory A. *Women Novelists of the 19th Century.* 1923

Batho, E. C., and Dobree, Bonamy. *The Victorians and After.* 1938

Benson, E. F. *Charlotte Bronte.* 1932

Bentley, Phyllis. *The Brontes.* 1947.

Birrell, Augustin. *Life of Charlotte Bronte.* 1887.

Bradby, G. F. *The Brontes and Other Essays.* 1932.

Braithwaite, W. S. *The Bewitched Parsonage.* 1950.

Bridges, Robert. *Collected Essays,* "The Poems of Emily Bronte." 1898.

Cecil, Lord David. *Early Victorian Novelists.* 1934.

Chadwick, E. A. *In the Footsteps of The Brontes.* 1914.

Chambers Encyclopedia of English Literature, "The Brontes." 1901.

Clarke, Isabel. *Haworth Parsonage.* 1927.

Cornish, Dorothy. *These Were The Brontes.* 1940.

Delafield, E. M. *The Brontes,* Their Lives Recorded by Their Contemporaries. 1935.

Dembley. *Key to The Bronte Works.* 1913.

Dimnet, Ernest. *The Bronte Sisters.* 1927.

Drinkwater, John. *Book for Bookmen.* 1927.

Gaskell, E. G. *Life of Charlotte Bronte.* 1857.

———. *Life of Charlotte Bronte.* Introduction and Notes by Clement Shorter. 1900.

Gosse and Garnett. *Cambridge History of English Literature.*

Green, Julian. *Suite Anglaise.* 1927.

Hanson, L., and E. M. *The Four Brontes.* 1949.

Harrison, G. E. *Methodist Good Companions.* 1935.
———. *The Clue to The Brontes.* 1948.
Hinkley, Laura L. *The Brontes, Charlotte and Emily.* 1945.
Kavanagh, C. S. *Symbolism of Wuthering Heights.* 1929.
Kinsley, Edith E. *Pattern for Genius.* 1937.
Lane, Margaret. *The Bronte Story.* 1953.
Law, Alice. *Emily Jane Bronte and The Authorship of Wuthering Heights.*
———. *Patrick Branwell Bronte.* 1923.
Leyland, F. A. *The Bronte Family with Special Reference to Patrick Branwell Bronte.* 1886.
Lucas, Peter. *Introduction to The Psychology of Wuthering Heights.* 1943.
Maeterlinck, Maurice. *Wisdom and Destiny.* 1905.
Mackay, Angus M. *The Brontes, Fact and Fiction.* 1897.
Margesson, Maud. *The Brontes and Their Stars.* 1928.
Masson, Flora. *The Brontes.* 1912.
Matthews, T. S. *The Brontes.* 1934.
Maugham, W. S. *Introduction to Wuthering Heights.* 1939.
Millmore, Royston. *A Brief Life of The Brontes.* 1947.
Moore, Virginia. *Life and Eager Death of Emily Bronte.* 1936.
Morgan, Charles. *The Great Victorians.* 1932.
Ratchford, F. E. *The Bronte's Web of Childhood.* 1941.
Raymond, Ernest. *In the Steps of The Brontes.* 1948.
Read, Herbert. *Reason and Romanticism.*
Reid, T. W. *Charlotte Bronte.* 1877.
Robinson, A. Mary. *Emily Bronte.* 1883.
Romieu, E., and G. *The Bronte Sisters.* 1931.
Saintsbury, George. *The English Novel.* 1913 ed.
———. *The Nineteenth Century.* 1896 ed.
Sanger, C. P. *The Structure of Wuthering Heights.* 1926.
Shorter, Clement. *Charlotte Bronte and Her Sisters.* 1895.
———. *Charlotte Bronte and Her Circle.* 1896.
———. *The Brontes: Lives and Letters.* 1908.

Shorter, Clement. *The Brontes and Their Circle*. 1914.

Simpson, Charles. *Emily Bronte*. 1929.

Sinclair, May. *The Three Brontes*. 1914.

———. *Introduction to The Works of The Brontes*. Everyman's Library.

Southwart, Elizabeth. The Bronte Moors and Villages from Thornton to Haworth. 1923.

Stephen, Leslie. *Hours in a Library*. 1879.

Sugden, K. A. R. *A Short History of The Brontes*. 1929.

Swinburne, A. *Miscellanies*. 1916.

Symons, A. *Figures of Several Centuries*. 1916.

———. *Dramatis Personae*. 1923.

Taine, H. *History of the English Novel*. 1909 ed.

Turner, J. H. *Haworth Past and Present*. 1879.

———. *Bronteana. Rev. Patrick Bronte*. 1932.

West, Rebecca. *The Great Victorians*. 1922.

Whately. *English Social and Domestic Life in the 19th Century*. 1897.

White, B. W. *The Miracle of Haworth*. 1937.

Willis, Irene Cooper. *The Brontes*. 1933.

———. *The Authorship of Wuthering Heights*. 1926.

Wilson, Romer. *All Alone: The Private Life and History of Emily Jane Bronte*. 1928.

Wise, T. J., and Symington, J. A., eds. *Shakespeare Head Bronte*, Their Lives, Friendships and Correspondence. 1932.

Woolf, Virginia. *The Common Reader: Jane Eyre and Wuthering Heights*. First series. 1925.

Wright, W. *The Brontes in Ireland*. 1893.

Yates, W. W. *The Father of The Brontes*. 1897.

Books: Emily Bronte

Wuthering Heights. Ellis Bell. With a biographical notice of Ellis and Acton Bell by Currer Bell. Editor's Preface by Currer Bell. 1850.

Five Essays in French. Emily Bronte. Introduction by F. E.
Ratchford. Trans. by Louise Nagel. 1948.
Poems. Currer, Ellis and Acton Bell. 1846.
Complete Poems of Emily Bronte. Edited by C. W. Hat-
field. Introduction by C. W. Hatfield. The Gondal Story
by F. E. Ratchford. 1941.
Complete Poems of Emily Bronte. Edited by Philip Hender-
son. 1951.

Books: Charlotte Bronte

Jane Eyre. Currer Bell. 1847.
Shirley. Currer Bell. 1849.
Villette. Currer Bell.
The Professor. Currer Bell. 1857.
Legends of Angria. Compiled by F. E. Ratchford. 1933.
Poems. C. E., and A. Bell. 1846.
Poems. Charlotte and Branwell Bronte. Edited by T. Wise
and J. A. Symington. 1934.

Books: Anne Bronte

Agnes Grey. Acton Bell. 1847.
The Tenant of Wildfell Hall. 1848.
Poems. C., E., and A. Bell. 1846.

Books: Branwell Bronte

Poems. Charlotte Bronte and Branwell Bronte. Edited by
T. Wise and J. A. Symington. 1934.
*Miscellaneous and Unpublished Writings of Charlotte
Bronte and Branwell Bronte.* Edited by T. Wise and J. A.
Symington. 1936.
The First Book of Horace Odes, trans. by Branwell Bronte.
Introduction by John Drinkwater. 1923.

Bronte Society Transactions

"The Brontes Today." Prof. Lascelles Abercrombie.

"The Work of Emily Bronte and the Bronte Problem."
J. Fotheringham.
"The Challenge of The Brontes." Edmund Gosse.
—"Local Color of *Wuthering Heights*." T. W. Hanson.
"The Brontes as Origins in the History of English Litera-
ture." George Saintsbury.
"Charlotte Bronte and Emily Bronte." Prof. C. E. Vaughn.
—"*Wuthering Heights*." Mrs. Humphrey Ward.
"The Bronte's Place in English Literature." R. B. Haldane.
"Contemporary Reviews of the First Bronte Novels." E. M.
Weir.
"Bibliography of Writings of the Bronte Family." Butler
Wood, compiler.

Periodical Material (Essays, Articles)

—Bloomfield, Louis. "Review of *Wuthering Heights*," *Time
and Tide*, March 1948.
Cautley, W. H. "Haworth Folk Who Knew The Brontes,"
Cornhill Magazine, July 1910.
Chadwick, E. C. "Emily Bronte as Lawyer." *The Bookman*,
November 1926.
Dodds, M. "Gondialialand," *Modern Language Review*,
January 1923, January 1926.
Grimshaw, Beatrice. "Emily and Charlotte Bronte," *John
O'London's*, October 1921.
Haldane, E. "The Brontes and Their Biographers," *The
19th Century*, Vol. 112, 1932.
"Letters of Patrick Bronte to Miss and Mrs. Burder,"
Sphere, August 1913.
Macdonald, F. "The Brontes in Brussels," *The Bookman*,
June 1894.
———. "Monsieur Heger," *The Bookman*, June 1896.
Mackay, Angus. "The Brontes at Cowan Bridge," *The
Bookman*, October 1894.

Mackay, Angus. "Emily Bronte," *Westminster Review*, August 1898.

Moore-Smith, Prof. C. "Brontes in Thornton," *The Bookman*, October 1904.

Nicoll, W. R. "Emily Bronte," *British Weekly*, October 1908.

Pritchett, V. S. *"Wuthering Heights,"* *The New Statesman*, June 1946.

Ratchford, F. E. "The Brontes' Web of Dream, *Yale Review*, 1931.

———. "War in Gondal," *Trollopian*, December 1947.

Smith, George. "The Brontes," *Cornhill Magazine*, 1873.

———. "In the Early Forties," *The Critic*, January 1901.

Swinburne, A. Review of Mrs. Robinson's *Emily Bronte*, *Athenaeum*, January 1883, June 1883.